The LIST

The LIST

This is the story of a courageous woman,
who would break free from danger and death,
risking her life and the lives of her children to get to freedom
– The Thailand Border!
Little did she know that God was guiding
her steps every moment of the way.

Manith K Sanchez

Editor Maxine Morarie (Mama)
Contribution by Raymond A Sanchez (Husband)

XULON PRESS

Xulon Press
2301 Lucien Way #415
Maitland, FL 32751
407.339.4217
www.xulonpress.com

© 2021 by Manith K Sanchez

Michael Richards, Contributing Writer, Updated May 22, 2019

Unless otherwise indicated, Scripture quotations taken from the King James Version (KJV) – *public domain*.

Paperback ISBN-13: 978-1-6628-2910-9
Dust Jacket ISBN-13: 978-1-6628-2911-6
Ebook ISBN-13: 978-1-6628-2912-3

Table of Contents

Introduction

One Snowy Morning

One snowy morning as I brought my car to a stop in the parking lot of the Pharmaceutical Company where I worked in Broomfield, Colorado, I sat in my car, waiting till it was time to go in. My eyes wandered here and there as the snow came down, and I hoped that it would stop soon. I had lived in America for over thirty years by this time, thirty winters, and I still disliked the snow! White snow was quickly covering the walkway and it was sure to be cold and slippery going from car to building. It gave me a chill just thinking about it, and I whispered to myself, *I don't like winter!* What a contrast from the memories of Cambodia, the picturesque, tropical-land I grew up in.

Stop complaining, Manith! I continued, *you have a thick, warm coat, a cozy stocking cap, and a new journal from your honorary-mama Maxine!* Looking down at the journal, I started planning how to share my story, smiling as I reread the challenge she'd written on the first page of her Christmas gift, "I want to see this notebook filled with the story of your life!" I felt a warm glow from the inside out, and I said, there is no one I would rather tell my story to than Mama Maxine! Checking the time, I saw that I had a good thirty minutes before braving the storm. I had decided to go into work early each morning, so that I could write a little every day.

Before putting pen to paper, I thought, *I want to share with mama about my country, my birth family, and my life – the good things as well as those that are painful to remember, but needful to include, in order to make it **my** story!*

Chapter One

Childhood

$\mathcal{C}$ambodia is a beautiful country, located at the far east side on the world map. It is surrounded by Thailand, Vietnam, and Laos. My village was very close to the jungle, not far from the border of Thailand, and very near the small town of Sisophon. Sisophon was a small community filled with good people with a high school, a middle school, a good-sized elementary school, and a winding bicycle path leading to them. This was the path my siblings and I, and most of the other children of our village, followed each morning. I loved going to school and being with my friends. The sun was always shining and the temperature, always warm. Every morning, you'd hear the sound of monks, chanting from the Buddhist temple the blessings from the Buddha. It didn't take long to reach the school, following the bicycle path; whether walking or riding a bike, it would only take ten or fifteen minutes.

Others used the path traveling from one point to another on business or to reach their farms. People hauling baskets and boxes of goods and produce to sell at the market met up with others coming to or returning from the market with the things they had purchased for that day's needs.

One could see clouds immersed between the mountains, exposing clear, blue skies overhead in the village. I can still remember how fresh and cool the air was in the early morning when the sun was just starting to shine. There is nothing like being awakened by cool, gentle breezes brushing your face, birds chirping and singing, and the aroma of jasmine tea! I would jump out of bed, wanting to be the one to carry a warm cup of tea out to the front porch for my grandmother.

She would smile her thanks as she sat down to enjoy it. During the school week, my siblings and I would scurry about the hallway looking for our shoes and schoolbooks. But on Saturday mornings, we would all come together to enjoy the morning sunrise with grandmother. It's a scene I'll never forget!

We sat on the front porch, enjoying the rice soup and dried meat that my mom cooked for breakfast. All around us the birds greeted the morning with songs that tuned-up our own senses for the day. Grandmother shouted loudly, "Good morning!" And, just as loudly, our neighbors returned their greetings.

My family, and most of the others in our village were farm-families. Our houses were stilt houses, built above ground with wooden walls and a metal roof. The profusion of colorful, fragrant flowers bloomed year-round everywhere you looked, and the loving, kind and supportive villagers were just as colorful and made it a wonderful environment to grow up in. Hot summers, a bit cooler at harvest time, made for only one type of weather report: pleasant, whatever the season.

This beautiful village sat at the side of a foothill surrounded by green mountains. Food was plentiful – coconut, mango, papaya and palm trees, groves of orange, tangerine, and banana trees, and fields of corn. There were many types of wild fruits – dragon fruit, cashews and others. Vegetable and small shrub gardens were planted around our homes. Cotton was a money crop that most farmers planted. Everywhere you looked, you'd see green plants growing from rich, moist soil.

Children, too, grew healthy and happy, as fruitful plants – where their parents, as rich moist soil, provided love and security for them. I was the oldest of my mother Cheiv Kein's three children. Her first marriage to our birth father Veasna Khoun ended in divorce. For reasons never revealed to us, he left her and his three little daughters (then three, one, and eight months old), never to return. It is to our step-father, Than Bour, that my sisters and I owe so much! We remain so grateful for the way he loved our mother and her little ones, and he never treated us differently than he did the other three girls and two boys he had with my mother after they married. He always referred to me as his oldest child. I considered him to be my real dad, and will always look at him that way.

As the oldest child, my dad would often invite me to take walks around our property just to enjoy how beautiful and fast-growing our garden was. We would get so excited and could hardly wait for the mangos, bananas or oranges to start ripening. We loved harvesting fruit from our own trees and vegetables from our own gardens. We depended solely on what we grew and the livestock that we raised - pigs, chickens, horses, cattle, and buffaloes.

My grandmother used to say, "We farmers must save everything – enjoy what we harvest and treasure the things we possess." She taught us not to waste anything, and knew all the ways to save, store, and repurpose. Nothing should be thrown out, if it could be used in any way. She believed when we owned something, we needed to maintain it, making it last as long as we could – this included our house, carriages, bicycles, tractors and other types of machinery. She taught each one of us how to be self-reliant, to plan, to carry out our plans, and understand all we could about life as farmers and our duty to each other and our community. Grandmother was the person in charge of our family's finances, and everything else that pertained to our well-ordered life.

As the oldest child I had a lot of responsibilities: I learned how to cook and farm from my mother and grandmother, and when my parents were working in the fields, I took care of my brothers and sisters. I managed my grandmother's store, which included the inventory of the products she sold and the handling of the income and expenses. I had been taught from a child to be honest, faithful, to respect others and myself – all qualities that helped in obtaining the trust grandmother had in me.

We children had to ask our grandmother for the money to buy school supplies, and even my parents had to have her approval and get money from her for farm equipment and other things they needed. She watched the money very closely and shared with no one where she hid the cash for family emergencies and rainy days! The time came, however, when she felt someone else needed to know those secret places, and she chose me to be that person! Because of her frugality there was always money to be had, and when neighbors and friends needed a helping hand, my parents and my grandmother would extend love and financial support, never asking to be paid back! I shall always be grateful for all the things I learned from my grandmother.

I can still hear her wise words in my memory. To my sisters and me she would say, "Women must learn how to cook. They need to be ready to care for themselves and their children should anything happen to their mates." And to my brothers, "You are going to be men. Be the kind of men who take care of themselves, and of their wives and children. Work hard, put your family first before yourself!" We all listened to her advice, because we knew that all of this wise counsel, all of her teachings, came from the great love she had for us. In turn we loved her and knew the only way to show her that love was to obey, respect and honor her.

I loved to ride my bicycle to school. Tall trees lined the bicycle path, and I enjoyed the shade and beauty they provided for trips to school. Some days, on my way home, I would stop and rest under the mango trees, lying down, looking up through the leaves, getting lost in their shelter. I used the mango trees also as a landmark – when I reached them, I knew I was getting closer. The bike path ended at a small pond formed by lakes alongside the main street.

We looked forward to our visits to the nearby country of Thailand during summer vacations from school. Besides being a good place to buy materials for our clothing, we would buy many other things we needed, because everything was cheaper across the border! It was worth the two-hour walk through the jungles, watching out for animals, snakes and other dangers, coming and going. We went as an entire family, because we would need everyone's help to carry our purchases home; however, only my parents and I bartered for the things we bought, for we were the only ones who knew enough of the Thai language. The others had the fun, we did the work, but we all benefited from the trip!

Sewing kept grandmother busy upon our return! We started each school year with new uniforms, and my parents always bought good material for them and for the other articles of clothing that growing children need. We were so proud of our new wardrobes. Our dad's farm-clothing wore out quickly and had to be replaced throughout the year. (Sewing is something I, too, am known for – another way grandmother influenced me!)

Of course, all of this took money, and we knew that it all depended on good crops – of rice, cotton, peanuts, sweet potatoes, and others. All of us children helped our father daily, working with him in the fields when needed throughout the farming season. I don't remember wishing we didn't have to work so hard; it was something we wanted to do. Helping our father was a privilege and made us feel close to him.

Our home was always full of commotion with children everywhere. There were eight of us children, two boys and 6 girls, but it didn't end there. My parents had made room for quite a few adopted children, as well. That is why my father built a large home for us with twelve bedrooms. There was a balcony that wrapped around the house. We enjoyed that balcony so much! Once or twice a month, my dad would hold the village meeting at our home. The villagers liked to get together to socialize and share hearts, and appreciated my parents' ready hospitality.

My parents' generosity extended to our community as they joyfully invested in helping others by giving and sharing from their stock of goods and plentiful harvests. You'd think they would have worried about how they were going to make it year after year, but if they did, they never put that burden on their children. I never heard them talking about how they were going to make it, but only about their concern for others. I am amazed at their acts of love, their kindness and how they reached out to the people in our village.

We were very fortunate to be among the children *who could* attend school; many families could not afford to give their children an education, and struggled day after day just to get by. It took money to keep a child in school. Even in my family, we children had to choose between school and farming. I chose to go to school where I could learn and explore new things. (And even today, I value learning about new things, and treasure all the knowledge that I accumulate.) Though I felt sorry for some of my brothers and sisters whose choice after elementary school was to farm, I imagine they might also have felt sorry for me – they got to be with my Dad all the time, while, as they saw it, I slaved away in high school! Whether school or farm was what we chose, we were all proud of our accomplishments.

I did very well in school and made many friends throughout the twelve years dedicated to my education. During school breaks, however, I joined my siblings, and we were Dad's farmhands – it was especially necessary when harvest time came! Bringing in the crops, getting them ready for market, took all the help he could get. Though much of it was sold, a good amount was saved for our yearly supplies, and this also took many hands!

We are a very close-knit family to this day and have always supported and shared what we have with each other. We were raised with boundaries and rules, a structure that made living together easy. Each one contributed to this well-run household – knowing what was expected of him/her, and cheerfully performing that task the best that he or she could.

You have already heard a lot about how much we all loved grandmother – she was always there to help us with our problems, and it didn't take long after sharing them with her until solutions were found, and our problems were no longer problems! "Be strong," she'd say, "And watch over each other." We admired her strong personality and were sure that she could protect us from anything!

Grandmother was skillful as a farmer, and it was by emulating her that our father became good at what he did. It is amazing how they could predict the weather at the beginning of each new year. When they agreed that it would be a good year, it was. And conversely, with their declarations of a bad year coming, they would think of other means to supply our family's most pressing needs. Whether good years or bad, my father and our wise grandmother never failed to guide us. Some years the harvest was so plentiful that our dad had to hire more people to help him gather it in. He was a very hard-working person, one who loved to provide for his family.

Hospitality was another of grandmother's strong points! If she noticed that children from a family with very little income were suffering, she would move them into our house, and help them back to health and well-being. The sick of the village would come to her, knowing that she would do all she could to help them. She welcomed other farmers and their families into our home – fed them and provided them with clothing. In fact, our home became the second home of many people in the village, and we thought of them as part of our family. When children would drop in on us, eating our food, and enjoying our family dynamics, they would tell us: "We wish we could stay here for good!" Our grandmother's love was something that they longed for, and many were taken under her wings, and from her, learned to be loving and kind as well. Some of the children she adopted actually did live with us year-round – enjoying my grandmother and my mother's cooking and helping my father in the fields. We went to school together, played together, swam across the river together, fished together, and proudly brought our catch home for grandmother to fry for dinner - it made us so proud! It was as though my parents were bringing up all the village children – there were so many eating and sleeping at our house! We would fight and squabble as siblings do and make each other cry, then make up, and soon be laughing again!

The bonds we formed were lasting, and this made our parents very happy. Not all homes had the same unselfish, all-inclusive way of doing things as was found in our home, nor did they have parents and grandparents working together in unison like ours. Setting goals and achieving them, sharing and reaching out to those who had less, was what was modeled to the many children that enjoyed our home.

And as for the "real" children of the family, we are all thankful that we were born to such good parents and taught by an honored and beloved grandmother like ours. We loved seeing how highly respected they were by the many adopted children they loved and embraced over the years. Love is a powerful thing.

If I were to describe the farming communities in Cambodia in one concise sentence, it would be this: We villagers were as close as though we were one family, living together under one roof!

Chapter Two

Lofty Goals

Grandmother always wanted the best for us kids, especially for me. In fact, her aspirations for my future were shared by the whole family. I was honored by this, and didn't want to let them down. I began to set goals for myself, knowing that the way to success was to keep reaching those goals. I had been successful in elementary and middle school, but soon found out that high school was going to be harder than I thought. But I buckled down and managed to do well there also.

I didn't want to pursue a life-career in farming, like my father and his before him. So, I set a career goal for myself: obtain a degree in business.

Grandmother, of course, was all for this choice and told me, "Whatever you want, set your heart upon it, never give up, and you will succeed! It all starts with a 'bright-education' – whatever you store in your brain, stays there until you die, and no one can steal it from you!"

But the greatest encouragement of all was when she confided, "Manith, I have faith in you! You can do it!"

My parents had their own way of saying the same thing: "Hard work pays off, no matter what you want for your life!"

My dad saw everything through the lens of his own occupation and would say, "Good crops come from hardworking people." My parents and grandmother were behind my lofty goals, and I wanted to make them proud.

Besides my career choice, I had another goal and that was to marry a well-educated and prosperous man, who could give me a better life than I had known in the small village I grew up in.

And then, the secret training, and the secret meetings began! The goals I had set for myself were greatly affected when a vicious goal-killer superimposed itself on all of us. Though I knew nothing about communism and wars, my parents did, and for many years they lived in fear of them; this great secret was kept from their children so as not to disturb us.

At the end of my twelfth grade, it was announced at our high school that a new requirement for graduation was to complete "The Protection Program." We would all be trained militarily so that in case of war we could defend our country. The training would include learning how to fight and use weapons such as hand guns, as well as M-16's and machine guns. A special military team was arriving to train us.

I couldn't wait to get home to tell my parents about this new program that I'd have to complete to graduate. I noticed the knowing look they exchanged, and thought, they've been expecting this!

Something about their reaction made me uneasy, and I became very concerned about the probability of war and how this would affect me as a person with goals - fighting enemies and reacting angrily was just not how I'd been brought up. And yet, would it really be necessary to protect our country? And from whom?

When the special military team arrived, regular classes were suspended, and the indoctrination began. "You students need to learn how to be soldiers and how to be strong. You must learn how to shoot and maintain guns of all kinds. This is not only a requirement for graduation, but an obligation to your country."

From that point on, they told us, our whole concentration must be on the program that was being introduced at our school.

It was as though we had all enlisted in the army, and our training went on with days, weeks, and months of practice, and we had no idea when it was going to end! Slowly many students began to take on the personalities of trained soldiers. I noticed that some of my classmates carried their guns out in public, and even into their homes, showing off to their parents and siblings.

And then, it wasn't only 'The Protection Program' in the high school where military talk and training was going on, but the men of the village began meeting to discuss contingency plans if war threatened our village. My dad seldom attended these meetings, but when he did, he would come home in a quiet and meditative mood. I never asked him about the meetings, for I knew that it would upset him. The fathers of the village had kept their meetings secret, because they didn't want their wives and children to worry or be afraid. Oh, the terrible secret of a coming war was fast reaching its revelation!

Many of the things we were taught in 'The Protection Program' were to be kept from our parents, which troubled me! I tried to comply, but finally, I couldn't keep it from my parents any longer. I let them know exactly what was going on at school and what they were teaching us! And then, my dad decided to share with the family what was going on in the secret meetings in our village.

He gathered us together and told us that some of our nation's leaders were embracing communism, and that one day we would have to escape as a family! "We need to start preparing for the day we will vacate our village! We need to have ready adequate supplies of medicine, food and clothing so that in case something really bad happens, at a moment's notice, we can leave. Meanwhile let us continue just as we are – but cautiously."

Would we escape to Laos, Vietnam, or Thailand, I wondered?

Grandmother spoke up and said, "I think we should go to Thailand. We have relatives there that would help us. It would take us longer to reach Vietnam, it is too far north, and Thailand is closer. And when we go, we must keep together and not get separated."

My dad's concern about the training I was receiving at school bothered him more and more each day. He kept watch on everything going on in the village, and would ask me about what was going on at school. When I would tell him, it made him very sad. He asked if he could train with the students, but the military team would not allow adults to join the training.

Dad would tell us kids, "Please trust me, and let me deal with what is happening. Don't worry and be upset. We'll find a way out!" And then he'd come up with possible things we could do, where we could go, and how we could escape.

He felt that one of the ways I could escape was to go to America as an exchange student. He had applied for this already, but we were still waiting to hear back. When I heard the good news that one of my high school classmates, A-Pichh, would be leaving Cambodian for America as an exchange student, I was very happy for her and excitedly anticipated hearing that I, too, was approved.

A-Pichh came by to share her happiness with me, and told me it was not too late. She knew how much I wanted a career in business, and assured me that America was the ideal place for that! "Don't give up, Manith," she encouraged.

"I hope I am accepted, but even if I can't go to America, at least I can find some place in Cambodia to pursue my dream," I responded. "My dad has already turned in the form and I'm looking forward to hearing good news, too. With all that's going on, I am anxious to get out of Cambodia. I keep telling myself to be patient, to wait and not to give up hope. It would be so nice to go to college in a more peaceful country."

I tried to stay calm, and volunteered to help my dad with the soon-coming harvest, but couldn't help but wonder what I would do if something happened in the village before I got the approval.

We were all worried and scared, and escaping was our focus every moment of every day. We had frequent talks as a family about being ready and not trusting anyone outside of our own family. "Keep your eyes open, watch for what goes on around you when you're out and about. And you must stay inside at night!" our parents would warn us.

People would come up missing, and town leaders were worried. We knew the capital of Cambodia was surrounded by communists and we heard that hundreds of people were being killed. When more people went missing from our village, we wondered if the communists had not already infiltrated our peace-loving community, though secretly.

People would say, "Communists are living in our village! Be careful what you say and what you do!"

One of the village chiefs and his wife disappeared just a few days after village meetings were stopped. This was very bad news. We hoped they were safe, but we had no way of finding out, and we knew that they could have been killed. The communists had been concentrated in the north, but were now moving south, converging on people from every direction. We had been noticing new people in the village who were standoffish and hard to get to know. We began to see people standing around in groups of three or four not too far from our house.

"Watch them closely," Dad would say, "and if they approach you, stay quiet, do not make noise. If they try to engage you in conversation, excuse yourself and head for home."

Our comfortable, beautiful village was fast becoming a dangerous place to live! Killings were becoming common, and the whole situation, very serious.

How strange to see our grandmother so concerned and frightened! "We must leave the village and go to Thailand," she kept insisting to my father.

"Not yet, Mother," he would respond. "Now's not the right time. We will get killed if we go too soon." He knew that there were two platoons of soldiers at the border to prevent people from entering Thailand.

We gave up hope of my moving on to college as an exchange student in America. All of that was put on hold, because of the more pressing need of escaping from the communists who had taken up residence among us!

Chapter Three

Arranged Marriage

My grandmother and parents told us that things were settling down somewhat, and though the new chief had given permission for people to return to their normal activities, that didn't mean all of our freedoms were returned – we must still be careful and lay low – not do anything that would make us conspicuous!

I didn't know until a little later, however, how conspicuous I was about to become!

The next family gathering had to do with me, and what was announced made me feel a tremendous loss of freedom, lowering of goals, forfeiting of a higher education, and separation from all that I had loved and held dear.

I knew all about arranged marriages, but because my parents had been encouraging me all along to have my own goals and to work toward them, I assumed I would be excused. I was wrong. Very matter-of-factly they let it be known that Manith would be getting married soon. I had no idea who I was going to marry, but they made it very clear that my job was to cooperate with their plans, and to make my parents and my grandmother happy.

I realized that the impending danger of war in my country, though somewhat dormant, may have had something to do with this sudden decision. One way I could honor them, they informed me, would be to agree to marry! Obedient daughter that I had always been, I agreed outwardly, but my heart was in conflict.

It was my dad who explained to me how the arrangement had come up. "A marriage proposal came out of the blue from a family in the city. We talked it over with your grandmother, and thought perhaps it would be better for you to marry now, before war breaks out."

They thought marriage was best for me, but I certainly did not, yet I didn't let them know how overwhelmed I felt. Everywhere I went, the news was bad about Cambodia - rumors of a take-over by the communists was all people talked about as they hurriedly made plans to escape. And now, on top of all that was happening, I was to marry, move away to a city, and abandon all my goals! It was almost more than I could stand! Not one thing about this traditional type of marriage pleased me.

My father read the facial expressions on my face as he talked, I knew that he knew what I was saying was different from what I was feeling! Usually he was quick to understand and to reason with me – this time, he just came right out with it: "Manith, it's done. We already accepted the proposal from the family in the city."

What he also meant was that the groom and his family would pay for everything, but I must be a virgin! As was the custom, the day after we married his parents would check this out! If there was no blood, it would mean I had lost my virginity before marriage and his parents would return me to my parents who would then be obligated to pay them back for everything they'd invested in the wedding. This would also result in my being shunned by my family, and I would have to leave my village.

When all this was explained to me, grandmother attempted to encourage me. "Before things get worse," she said, "while there's still time, before war begins, we want you to have a nice wedding."

The last thing I wanted, however, was *a nice wedding* and then being forced to live far away from my family. And when things did get worse, as everyone expected, the last thing I wanted was to be under the dominion of a husband and his family; people I did not know with customs that I did not yet understand – they were city people, and I was a farmer's daughter. I said to myself: I think my wedding is going to be more of an escape for my family rather than a time of happiness for me – planning wedding festivities will help them to forget, however briefly, the threat of war! Whether I am happy or sad doesn't seem to figure into the equation! I am soon to experience another kind of threat. Our country is about to be captured by the communists, and I, by an arranged marriage.

That night when I went to bed after learning my fate, I couldn't turn my mind off! What my family should be celebrating, I told myself, is that I have just graduated from high school! Grandmother always told my siblings and me that having a good education was very important! She'd tell me to be someone the younger children could look up to as a role model. I had taken that very seriously and was always on hand to help them to learn to read and write, even those that chose farming over school – and now their role model was to be snatched from them? It didn't make sense!

But I always came back to this: I need to obey – that is what is expected of me!

And so it was, that soon after my high school graduation in 1976, I had my beautiful, but dreaded, wedding!

Sorn, the groom, was 25 and I, the bride, was 19 years of age. The day of the wedding we were dressed in elaborate garments reminiscent of a king and queen. Our attendants were made up of two each of my brothers and sisters, and two each of his brothers and sisters. Their garments were also beautiful. Special attention was given to his parents. My mother, father, and grandmother were also honored. And almost everyone in our village attended.

The festivities went on for seven days, with feasting and drinking a special whiskey, made by my grandmother. My dad killed one cow, three pigs, and, each day another twenty chickens were killed – the vegetables from our own garden provided the side dishes. Food was plentiful. Fruit bowls were kept filled with oranges, mangos, papaya, nectarines, pomegranates and pineapple!

I found my goals very hard to lay down! All the while I was going through the motions of celebrating my marriage, I was thinking about what would not be celebrated: a college degree, the career I had planned for. I had accepted the fact that I would not be going to college in America as an exchange student, but I could have attended the college in our small village. I wanted to run with each step I took, but that would dishonor my family; arranged marriages were an intricate part of Cambodian tradition. I probably wasn't the first that dreaded marrying a person she didn't know, and I knew I wouldn't be the last – so, I stoically kept taking the steps required of me!

I did a lot of self-talking through it all, and my spirits lifted a little when I told myself, *Manith, you are going to be okay! The man you are marrying is well-educated, and works for the government! You have always loved learning about new things, and taking challenging situations in your stride! Your husband will introduce you to city life and, who knows, you might grow to love each other. Some parents arrange the marriage when the child is very young – and such children have to include an early marriage in their goals! Thankfully that didn't happen to you. Has your grandmother ever put you in danger? Have your mother and father ever asked you to do something that didn't turn out well in the end? Of course not!*

My parents and grandmother were so proud of me, and as they talked with our friends during the celebration, they always pointed out – *the groom is well-educated, he works for the government, and lives in the city!* I knew that the whole thing, the ceremony, feasting, and how beautiful I must have looked, pleased them. And that should have made me happy, but I felt obligated to accept a husband for whom I felt no attraction, and I doubted that he felt any love for me either. I had to face the challenges before me: cutting ties with my wonderful parents and grandmother, laying down my text books, picking up all the responsibilities of a housewife, and depending upon and obeying my supposedly well-educated husband.

We left the village a week after the wedding and headed to the city.

Things were not bad in the beginning, my husband worked as a forest ranger, and I worked at home – going to market, cooking, washing clothes, cleaning house, and doing all I could to be a good wife. I took special pains with his clothing, ironing them and putting them away very carefully. The adjustment from farm girl to city house-wife was easier than I thought, and since I didn't work outside the home, I had plenty of time for everything. Each day I anxiously awaited his arrival from work with an immaculately clean house, and the smell of good food. It took a while, but I soon learned to cook the food he liked best, giving special attention to our dinner meals.

I began to relax a little and thought, *being a housewife is not so bad, and I rather like keeping house and making my husband happy.* But I had to admit that I felt lonely until he would get home from work each night.

One thing I soon noticed about city life, was that everyone did their own thing, and you didn't get to know the people that lived around you. Not at all like waking up in our village, sipping jasmine tea in the morning and calling out greetings to our friends! I soon learned my way around the city, but not into the hearts of people! No one to chatter with or to laugh with when something was funny. I didn't even know my next-door neighbors, even though our houses were built very close together – so close that at times I felt claustrophobic. In our village we dressed humbly, but here, no one went out on the street in casual clothes – *dressing up is something I need to learn*, I admonished myself, *so that my husband won't be ashamed of me!* My ready smile as I passed people on the street had to stop! I wasn't in the village where I knew everyone and it would have been rude not to smile and be friendly in passing. No one here wants to be my friend, was my conclusion, and my smiles and greetings make them uncomfortable!

The things I shared above, were only first impressions! Eventually I learned how to dress, and how to fit in. And then, a new challenge – motherhood! Three months into my marriage I found myself pregnant – I was surprised and very happy at the same time. As most mothers, I looked forward to meeting and welcoming a new family member – excited to know whether it would be a boy or a girl! Eager to share my life with this little person, I started collecting materials and sewing baby clothes – something Grandmother had made sure I would be able to do, and I smiled to think how pleased she would be with the sweet little baby garments I created. I focused on taking good care of myself to prepare for the birth of our child.

But, my husband, on the other hand, seemed to be indifferent. In fact, after six months of marriage, I realized he could care less about me or becoming a father! His commitment to me and to our marriage began to change.

The first time he didn't come home after work, I sat up and waited for him. We didn't have a telephone, so I knew there was no way he could call. I was sure something had happened to him – maybe he was hurt, maybe he'd abandoned me – all kinds of possibilities presented themselves – and I was overcome with worry. I'd stare out the window, hoping to catch sight of him. But nothing. Finally, it got so late that after leaving a plate of food on the table and clearing the kitchen, I went to bed, but I couldn't sleep. I got up in the morning, hoping to find him sleeping somewhere else in the house. He was nowhere to be found!

This happened often, and sometimes he'd stay away two or three days at a time! Other times he would come home, smelling of alcohol. I wanted to confront him to find out if he was in some kind of trouble at work, but I couldn't muster the courage to ask. He never offered an excuse, but instead totally ignored me.

Week after week, late at night, he'd arrive drunk. I lived worried and scared. And then, one day I asked, "Why are you coming home late at night, smelling of alcohol?"

He started to yell and scream, calling me names, slamming doors and kicking the walls! And then he attacked me! He slapped my face, pushed me up against the kitchen wall and punched me in the stomach. I fell down on the kitchen floor and begged him to stop hurting me. "I'm pregnant, please don't hurt our baby," I tried to reason with him.

Days, weeks and months went by, and he stopped talking to me, but kept up the physical abuse. I would cry myself to sleep at night, hoping the next day would be different. Days would go by when he would not come home, and alone in the house, I would try to figure things out! What should I do, I asked myself. Whatever love I had had for him was gone, and all I cared about now was the baby, and keeping it safe.

I did learn that he was gambling, and it had gotten out of control, the reason why he was drinking so heavily. He must have been angry with himself, his debt, his addictions – but I became the target of his anger. There had never been evidence of love for me, only lust. No doubt this marriage had been a mistake from the start!

I began to have my own anger – towards the man I had married, and towards my parents and my grandmother who had arranged this marriage! I had never been slapped or struck before, never disciplined in this way as a child. I had no idea such marriages as mine existed! I'd never seen my parents fight or scream at each other. My father was always kind and in control, and I'd never seen my mother sad or resentful. The only model of marriage I had seen up to this time was something beautiful. What have I done wrong? Am I at fault in any way? I'd ask myself, *If I do this, or if I do that, could things get better?* Maybe I was too young and inexperienced to be married. Tons of questions and self-accusations came to my mind, but none of the answers!

The pain, mental and physical, that I lived with, made me regret the whole marriage, and yet I didn't know how to get out of it! There was, as far as I could see, absolutely nothing I could do about the gambling, drinking, or abuse. I had no friends, no family close by, that I could ask for counsel.

One thing I had learned was how to obey, how to be submissive, but should one be submissive to a person that caused you mental and physical pain? The bruises on my body seemed to scream, NO! What about the baby? Wasn't I responsible to protect it? To this question, the bruises on my body seemed to scream – YES. All the while, Cambodian tradition and customs screamed: You MUST be a submissive wife; you MUST bear the pain; you MUST learn to be strong through it all; you MUST overlook the lonely nights and neglect, the drinking and gambling. Remember, your husband is your boss!

So, Cambodian housewife that I was, day after day, I would make sure dinner was ready, and on the nights when he did come home, I would serve him. More often than not, despite my efforts, I would stare at our wedding pictures over and over till I would face the truth, he's not coming home, and I would lie down on our bed, alone in the house, and cry myself to sleep.

And then I seemed to come to my senses! I had married for better or for worse, but my 'husband' had not. Though tradition reminded me to accept the rules and customs of our culture, it didn't mean I should put up with my situation, nor ignore the safety of my child. I had done all the things a Cambodian wife should do, and did not talk back to the man I had married – but in return for this, he showed me in every way he could that he was not a husband to me.

Had he been a proper husband, he would have taken me to live with his family for six months to a year, but he broke with tradition, and never did have us move in with his parents who would have guided us. He would not have gotten away with how he was treating me if we were with his family, and he could have learned the proper way to treat and live with a wife. His actions led me to understand that the expectations he had for this marriage were: his wife would be his slave, all decisions would be his, all the possessions would be his, there would be nothing in common, and she must give up all rights and freedoms.

Now I realized why it was that many city men liked to marry country girls. They could take them off to the city, treat them any way they wanted, and his wife's parents would be none the wiser! Besides that, they knew that country people are very honest, committed and obedient.

I felt somewhat resentful of my parents. Had they investigated the man I would marry? Did they know anything about him before the wedding other than he's well-educated, he's from the city and works for the government? I'm sure they thought they were placing me in good hands, but they had taken a lot for granted! I'm sure my parents never would have allowed me to marry anyone who would be so abusive, I told myself. I knew divorce would not be possible for a wife, while a man is allowed five wives or more if he so desires.

I'd been going through this for two months and was now in my eighth-month of pregnancy. We hadn't paid the rent for two or three months, and I wondered what I would do if they made us move out. Much of the time, I had no money for groceries, and wondered how we were going to survive in the city without crops or gardens of our own. Sometimes I wanted to run away from him, but I had nowhere to go, and knew no one who would take me in!

He finally had a talk with me about our situation – omitting the fact that our debt was due to his betting and gambling loans! "We have no money for the birth of the baby," he said, "and I think you should go back to your parents."

I was so happy to hear him say that! He would allow me to go back home; oh, if I only had the money.

One day, while my husband was at work, I heard the voice of a woman, calling at my door.

"Hello," she said, "I'm your neighbor next door. I keep hearing a man yelling and a woman crying, and I'm concerned."

I tried to hide the bruises, but as she talked to me, I could see that I couldn't hide them from her. "Tell me how you got those bruises on your face," she asked.

I tried to change the subject, but she persisted, "Show me the rest of your bruises!"

When I did, she said, "I think your husband has been hitting you. That is not right, and especially when you are pregnant! I want to help you."

We talked some more, and then, before she left, she asked if I was going to be okay. I smiled and said that I would be.

The next time she came for a visit, she noticed fresh bruises on my face, and said, "How did you get these new bruises?"

"Oh, I ran into the corner of the bathroom door," I lied.

She believed me, and told me I needed to be more careful, and that when you're pregnant your balance is off and it makes one a little clumsy. I fixed some tea, and we had a good visit, and she told me she'd be seeing me again.

Another time when she came over (I think to check up on me and make sure I hadn't gotten hurt) she asked me, "Do you want to take a walk and get some fresh air?"

"I'd like that very much," I was quick to say. And from then on we would take walks. Oh, it was wonderful to have someone to walk and talk with, and to know there would be someone checking on me after my husband left for work. However, I never told my husband about my new friend.

Somehow, just knowing she was there for me, gave me the courage to make an important decision – I would not just lie down and take it anymore when my husband would become abusive.

One day he came home from work in a terrible mood. Usually, through fear, I wouldn't speak up when he'd start the verbal and physical abuse. But this time, I had the courage to do so. I said, "I will not allow you to hit me anymore. You may accidently hit the baby, and I have to protect it."

My kind friend reached out to me! "You need your parents, and so does that baby," she smiled, and handed me a bus ticket, "Go home, little friend. Leave your angry husband!"

Without a word to him, early one morning right after he left for work, I went to the bus station, and soon was on my way home! I didn't know for sure how my family would feel about my return. But when I arrived at the village and walked into our home, they were all overjoyed to see me, as I was them! When my mother and grandmother saw the bruises on my face and body, they knew why I'd come, and they opened their arms to me! The joy that gave me started to cure all the pain and hurting I'd been through.

I would never again go back to my husband, and after I told them why I'd left the city and returned to our village, they agreed. We all forgot the other member of the arranged marriage, and looked forward to meeting the child that I carried home with me in my tired and bruised body! I needn't have worried about how I would be received at home, for my parents and grandmother welcomed me. I looked at the smiling faces of my siblings, and knew they, too, welcomed having their oldest sister back home where she belonged! Though a bruised role model, I perhaps modeled for them a wife that had the courage to do what was right for herself and her baby.

Chapter Four

Becoming a mother

How calm and peaceful it was with my parents, siblings and grandmother! I knew they were still concerned about me, and worried about my marriage, but we were all looking forward to the little baby that would soon be joining us - I was in the ninth month of my pregnancy and eager to hold my baby in my arms.

It had taken me a while before I felt comfortable enough to share with my family what had happened in more detail, and how different and hard I found life in the city to be. I let them know about the abuse. I told them about our debts, and my husband's addiction to gambling and alcohol. I felt ashamed and sorrowful, and would cry as I explained why I had to leave – that we were about to be evicted. I hoped they would understand and not find fault with me.

The painful memories never seemed to go away completely, especially at night when I'd mull things over in my mind as I tried to go to sleep. Maybe one day they will fade, I told myself, after my baby is born!

The physical wounds healed, but the emotional ones took longer! I kept telling myself to be strong – for the baby!

I had allowed others to make decisions for me, when it was I who had to live with them, and for this I had only myself to blame! When I realized this, a new strength came upon me and with it, the determination to never again agree blindly to the decisions of others – no matter how much I loved them.

For the first time I realized that grandmother was idealistic in her counsel. Talking with her one day about my marriage, I said, "Grandmother, you see things through different eyes than mine. Your counsel would have been perfect had I married someone here in our village. But you have no idea what people from the city are like, nor the loneliness one feels, walking among crowds of people who do not know you, or care what happens to you. And the intense loneliness when the person you are married to dishonors you day after day – not talking to you, not planning with you, indifferent to your needs. Sometimes Sorn would stay away for days at a time. I'd be sure he had abandoned me; and then, when he'd come home drunk, screaming, punching and slapping me, I would wish he had abandoned me!"

She would listen quietly, trying to conceive of such a thing, saying nothing and withholding her counsel. And I would continue, "The memories haunt me, grandmother, but I try to be brave! I think I was a very good wife. I never neglected our home. I was faithful to Sorn and served him. I tried to hide the bruises so that he'd have a good name. I'm sure I did nothing to destroy our marriage. I think you would have been proud of me, but I had to protect my baby and that's why I came home."

I was so happy when the family's focus turned to the baby! I had tried to engage my husband to talk about our child – but he was totally disinterested even when I'd suggest names. Now everyone had an opinion and we'd all laugh together and it was wonderful. But at night, in my bed, I'd cradle my belly, hoping the growing little bump had not been harmed by the blows to my stomach!

I wondered if Sorn had any regrets, or even gave us a thought! The tears that would come to my family's eyes when they remembered what I'd suffered, showed me that they cared, and this comforted me and gave me permission to cry also. I knew they were sorry for the marriage they had arranged for me to such a cruel man. I knew that my pain was their pain, and they kept assuring me how good it was to have me back home with them.

One day, after I'd first returned, my father said tenderly, "Welcome home, sweet child! I will never let you go back to your husband again. You and your baby will be supported by our family. It will be born where it is loved – with us! Just focus now on your health so that you will be strong when your baby is born." Oh, how wonderful to be loved and cherished!

"Your father told me that he would never trust another word that comes out of your husband's mouth," my mother told me, "and if Sorn ever does come back to get you, he'll have to go through your father!"

Grandmother began all of the ancient preparations for birthing time and for the baby. Day after day she'd go out into the jungle to gather the roots and herbs that she would need – ginseng, ginger, turmeric, galangal and many others. As she always did, she prepared to take charge of everything pertaining to the arrival of the new-born child.

A beautiful baby girl was born in 1976, healthy, precious, and unharmed! Oh, how relieved I was. I named her Kechara, which meant first child. Everyone was happy, and welcomed my baby girl into the world. She was a gift from heaven; we sang songs and rejoiced. She brought happiness to our family. I felt so blessed when I saw how perfect she was. Everyone wanted to hold her and to predict her future! With all the young aunts and uncles in the family she was passed from one arm to another –and I feared this adorable baby girl would be royally spoiled!

Despite all the attention she received from others, grandmother never let her out of her sight. It was she who would feed her and rock her to sleep most of the time, while my mother kept busy, making clothes for her first grandchild, so that everything would fit perfectly as she grew. She enjoyed watching my siblings vie for turns to hold Kechara, and she just kept sewing clothes of many different colors. She would even bring out clothing she'd saved from her own babies, and would tell us just who had worn them before her sweet granddaughter did! How pretty my baby girl looked all the time and I loved her very much.

One day, my sweet little daughter had just fallen asleep in my arms after nursing! I sensed someone was near and quickly looked up, and there was her father standing on our doorstep. He walked toward me, smiled, and said, "Hello, Manith, how are you?"

With icy fear, I didn't return his greeting, but alarmed, called out, "Dad! Grandmother! Come quickly!"

I heard them running toward us and realized I was holding the baby too tightly so that he could not take her from me.

"I'm not going to harm you," Sorn tried to assure me with a calm voice. But when my father walked into the room, and Sorn saw the look he gave him, he must have realized that my family had heard how cruelly he had treated me!

He began to apologize. "I'm so sorry I was not here when my baby was born. I appreciate everything you've done for Manith and the baby."

"Your baby has a name," my father told him sternly. "It is Kechara!"

Sorn looked at me and smiled in approval, but he looked back at my father. Calmly but firmly my father told him, "Manith will no longer live with you in the city, Sorn. She and Kechara will remain here with us as part of our family."

And then my parents, grandmother and I faced him with steeled gazes, silently forcing him to think about all the ways he had failed in the marriage. My father finally said, "Manith had no choice, but to protect her child and come home to us. And she has told us that you even asked her to return to our village, isn't that so?"

Sorn didn't deny any of this.

"The baby and I need my family and we are thriving here. I do not need you," I told him.

After a time of talking, it was decided that I would be released from the marriage. I would live with the most important people of my life in the village I had grown up in, and he would go back to the city alone and continue working for the State.

Some months later, my dad told us, "Things are really worsening here in Cambodia, and we must leave the country. War is imminent. We must prepare."

I was very worried and curious to know more about what was going on and how it would affect our village, but my father told me, "I do not trust anyone in the village. People come up missing all the time and no one will say anything. We are not together as a village any longer. Everyone is suspicious, even of their neighbors. What we do now, we must do on our own!"

A few weeks later, Sorn showed up again. "We are at war – a serious one," he began. "The communists are flocking into northern Cambodia from Vietnam. They have demolished the capital and thousands of people have been killed. Soon every border will be blocked, and it will be impossible to escape. We will all be killed, if we don't do something!"

He looked at me and said, "I'd do anything to protect you and our baby, Manith. Let's be a family again."

31

My parents were skeptical, and didn't know if they could trust his words or not.

"Let me take Manith and Kechara back to the city," he pleaded with my father. "I know the government team there will help us, and give us a place to hide and we can keep abreast of communist activities. I've heard that small towns will be invaded first. They'll be searching for the well-educated: doctors, lawyers, school professors, nurses and government workers – and even high school graduates. They have the names of all of these on their LIST, and when found, they will be killed."

Sorn's words were convincing, so my father reluctantly let him take us with him, explaining, "This seems the best thing for you, Manith, and baby Kechara, especially if he can hide you in the city."

Knowing that we were already being surrounded by our enemies, and not knowing for sure who they were, left us feeling frightened and vulnerable.

"Sooner or later the Cambodia–Thailand border will be taken over by the communists," Sorn told us again. "That's why I want to get Manith and the baby far away from the village as soon as I can!"

How quickly things changed – I would be leaving my family behind once again, returning to the city I hated, with a husband I couldn't trust, and would have to go into hiding immediately.

Arriving in the city, we headed for the basement of the courthouse where there was a secret underground chamber where we could find refuge. Many people were hiding there already and I noticed it was stocked with canned goods.

I kept thinking of my final hours with my family. "Come with us," I had begged them!

"No," my father was quick to answer. "We will be fine. Don't worry. I'll find some way to keep us safe."

I knew he had already planned their escape into Thailand, and he said, "Manith, we will meet again someday in Thailand. But go now, while you have the opportunity. Escape to the city!"

"I'll do what you say, Father! And when this is all over, I will look for you in Thailand!"

"We might have to live in refugee camps," he said, "look for us there."

North Vietnam had been at war with the United States since 1965, but our father never said much about this. It wasn't so much that he wanted us to be in ignorance, but innocence was our best defense with the communists that were spreading about the country from northern Cambodia!

On our way back to the city, troubling thoughts invaded my mind: I don't know when I am going to see my parents and Grandmother again! This is the second time they have pressured me to go with this man, and I'm not sure I've done the right thing! It's hard to make a good decision when you're scared and confused! Then I would scold myself for worrying: *Father promised me we would meet again! Wars end! Maybe this one will end soon!*

But realistically I knew the likelihood of seeing my family again was very slim!

It seemed safe in the underground hide-away of the court house. Only government workers and their families were there, but it was very crowded. One day Sorn whispered, "Manith, I've found a small, abandoned dwelling not far from here where we can be alone. Shall we hide there?"

I agreed it would be better than hiding with so many people.

33

Kechara was now four months old and we were doing everything we could to ensure she wouldn't cry and give us away to the communist soldiers that patrolled the city.

Chapter Five

Explosions

*I*t was cloudy the morning that I looked out the window from our hide-away-house and saw a group of soldiers dressed in black uniforms, carrying guns, and marching down the street. I wondered where they had come from.

I had just sat down to nurse Kechara, when I heard a loud explosion. I looked out and saw flames of fire, and black smoke billowing into the air about a mile away. I could tell that some of the tall buildings visible from the deserted house we lived in had been blown up, and were now collapsing. The wind was blowing the debris-filled smoke in our direction, and it quickly became hard to breathe. In the sudden chaos, I heard loud and demanding shouts in front of our house: "Get out! Get out! Get out now!"

One of the soldiers rushed angrily into the house, and hurried past me. I was too shocked to say anything, but Sorn came running toward him and asked, "What is going on?"

The soldier kept shouting: "Get out!! Get out NOW!! If you don't, we will kill you!!"

Other soldiers had come in, and were pointing their guns at Sorn, and pushing him through the front door. I was scared, but ran after him, holding tightly to little Kechara.

They tied Sorn's hands behind his back with rope, and kept their guns pointed at his head. "Stay where you are!" they shouted. "Do you have any guns?"

"No," Sorn quickly answered, "we do not own any weapons."

They were leading my husband toward the street and I ran behind them and begged them to let me go with him, "We'll do whatever you want – just don't leave my baby and I behind!"

One of the soldiers untied Sorn's hands and then, pushed him away, shouting, "Leave immediately and don't come back!"

We were astonished and just stared at each other – communicating without words that we had no food, water or anything else for the baby! We hesitated for a moment, and looked back at the house!

"Get going! If we see you again, you will die! The communists have taken over Cambodia and there's a new regime!" the soldiers yelled.

The next look we exchanged was one of hopelessness – we took off running, as commanded, not knowing where we would go or what we would do. There were many people on the streets just like us! Their houses had been bombed, and they had dodged the grenades that had been thrown at them. Everyone was in shock. Men, women, and children - all were crying and sobbing.

Here and there, we'd hear someone calling to loved ones, trying to reconnect with them. Many of these were children, whose parents had been separated from them, or killed. Elderly people, frightened and weak, were trying to keep up with those of us running away. We kept hearing explosions – and when we looked back we saw flames coming from our neighborhood. Though we looked for familiar faces, we were so black from the mixture of smoke, sweat, and tears that we could not recognize anyone.

I was angry! How could these communist soldiers be so cruel? Their next targets were the vehicles, and small businesses – we saw them pouring gasoline on these, and setting them on fire! The smoke was so dense we could hardly see our hands before our faces, so Sorn and I held hands so we wouldn't get separated. It was getting very difficult to breathe – the combination of exertion with all the smoke from the fires made running hard, and we worried about Kechara. We held her little face toward our bodies to protect her from the smoke. We saw people who had collapsed from lack of oxygen, but because we'd be shot if we stopped to help them, we had to leave them to their fate – doubting that anyone would get them to medical help if indeed medical help still existed!

We could hear people calling out to each other, "Where are you? Where are you?" More and more people were getting lost, and were sobbing and wandering aimlessly. Many were angrily shouting: "Who are these people? Why did they do this to us?" Panicked teenagers were running here and there, looking for their parents and calling out their names! The elderly continued crying out for help, and no one stopped to help them. We had no leaders, no type of organization, just hopeless people running for their lives, with no idea where they were going!

Some became disoriented and would turn back, declaring to no one in particular, "I'm going home!" Only to hear, "You can't go home, keep running! You don't have a home, they've blown it up! And the soldiers will kill you if you go back!"

We kept walking farther and farther away before reaching the many acres of rice fields at the edge of the city. The day had come to an end, the sun was going down and it was getting dark, the exhaustion fueling a sense of apathy! The only thing we wanted now was a place to rest!

Sorn found us a secluded place at the bottom of a little slope. It wasn't till we sat down that we realized how sore our feet were!

We huddled together, hoping to stay warm. Falling asleep was no problem, but staying asleep was impossible! Every noise jarred us, and our little Kechara would not stop fussing. The night was cold, we had no blankets, and we were terrified; too close to the city to light a fire!

After the restless night, morning finally came and the fear of the communists, combined with the need for food and water, left us with only one thing to do – start out again, so we could get as far as we could from Battambong City!

We joined the others and walked in a sort of caravan, one after another all the next day! Some were crying, others became angry, but the emotion we all had in common was fear!

Trying to encourage myself, I thought, "Though we have nothing, we have one thing that cannot be taken away or destroyed, and that is our courage!" And I was sure that would have been my grandmother's counsel had she been there with us. I wondered where she, my parents and siblings were.

How could one human being treat another so badly? What kind of indoctrination did the communists receive to make them so hard-hearted? I could still hear in my mind my father warning us: "Communists kill anything that gets in their way. They shoot anyone who stands up to them or questions them. They have no mercy. Their one mission is to destroy Cambodia by wiping out its people!"

We walked aimlessly every day. Our main occupation was searching for water and food. We started to drink water from the rice fields even though we knew it was contaminated. We tried to catch frogs and small fish from the ponds we encountered along the way and ate them. We shared what we found with the elderly people who walked with us. Most of the evacuees were city people; they had no idea how to survive in the jungles. They had no idea what food was safe, nor how to find it. Those that had money would try to buy food from us, when they saw us eating.

People began forming smaller groups, and choosing alternate destinations. Some inquired of us where we were going, and joined our group. Those first few days our travels took us through one rice field after another. We had not yet come across any villages, and, remembering that the small villages were to be the first attacked, according to what my father had learned, we thought it was fortunate we hadn't. Though large cities were few in Cambodia, there were many towns and villages, relatively close together.

It sickened me when I reflected on our beautiful country being destroyed needlessly at the hands of the communists! I had never seen anything like this before. We plodded along, determined to find either a main road or a village, so we could finally leave the rice fields. I'm not sure how many nights we slept out in the open since leaving Battambong City before we finally caught sight of a village!

On that particular morning, we felt tired and weak when the sun was starting to rise – but we got up, prepared the food we'd gleaned the day before, and by mid-morning had set off on our journey to nowhere! "Maybe we'll come across a main road today and be able to find our bearings and discover where we are," Sorn commented.

There were more than ten of us traveling together, and someone in the group called out, "Look ahead! It's a village!"

We approached the town cautiously, hoping we wouldn't see any soldiers. The town was so quiet; we could see that it had been burned down, and appeared to be vacated. We saw no people, no soldiers, just a few live chickens pecking the ground for insects and worms. Here and there we would see a pig or a duck.

Sorn said, "Manith, we need to find whatever food there is to replenish our supplies and then move on as quickly as we can!"

We found some uncooked rice left in a small bag and a handful of dried meat. But when we came upon machine guns and machetes stored in one area of the village, we knew it had not been abandoned – soldiers would likely return any minute from whatever mission they were on!

"That's all we have time for, Manith, let's go!" Sorn hurried me off so that we would be gone when the soldiers returned and found we had raided some of their food. We made sure we were far enough away before we stopped to cook what we had found!

How delicious 'real food' tasted – rice and dried meat! Our hunger satisfied, we moved quickly through the tall, thick jungles where it would be easier to hide if the soldiers came upon us. I so appreciated my husband at that time as he took turns carrying Kechara, and looking after us.

We came into areas where we could hear in the distance sounds of gunshots and bombs exploding. With our stomachs full for the first time, we were able to pick up our pace. By this time, we kept pretty much to ourselves, our group was disintegrating, but we would suddenly come upon other groups of people, traveling through the jungles, no doubt fleeing from villages that had been attacked.

We were all alone, and had spent the night under a large tree. When we awoke in the morning we felt comfortable under the tree, and one of us suggested, "Let's build a little shelter under this tree and stay put for a while!" We gathered tree leaves, branches and some sturdy logs and built our makeshift cabin.

It rained really hard the next day, and we were happy that we'd done such a good job, for we stayed dry and warm in our temporary abode! The next morning, we sat out in the sunshine to warm up and took inventory of our sores and bruises. The ones on my feet were very painful, and we realized it had been a good decision to stay put for a while, to recuperate our energies. One day had blurred into another, and we had no idea how many nights and days we had been running; we needed this rest! We had settled on the edge of a rice field in the middle of nowhere. I even made pillows from straw, and when I would put Kechara to sleep I would put my head down on the prickly pillow, and snuggle her closely, amazed to have such a comfortable place at last!

But it wouldn't last! I would soon be imagining I was hearing shouting, gun fire, and explosions! And then, I would start missing the peaceful life I had lived with my parents in our village.

I must learn how to quiet the voices in my head, I would scold myself! (Sometimes, even yet, I hear the soldiers yelling and screaming and telling us, Cambodia now belongs to the communists – there's a new regime! Get out! Get out! Get out! Oh, how I hope I will never have to go through anything like that again!)

Grandmother once told me the story about when she and my grandpa had been robbed by some thieves from Thailand. "They came during the night and robbed us, taking everything they could get their hands on! Your grandpa fought back!" she told me. "But he lost his life trying to protect us – the thief shot him and he died in my arms from the wounds!"

When this story would come to my mind, I would tell myself, the soldiers forced us to leave our house, but we still have our lives! I'm so grateful we weren't shot like my grandpa! They told us to go and never come back, but in truth, I wouldn't want to go back to the city where we saw houses, buildings, and schools burning to the ground. But I do wish we could go back to my village! And if we do go back, I hope it hasn't been burned to the ground, I hope my family is alive and well. I hope that one day life will be back to normal. But how could that be? The communists are demolishing everything they come across!

Chapter Six

Surviving & Hiding

*M*onths passed and we continued living in our crude little dwelling in the jungle at the edge of a rice field. We survived by eating fish, snails and frogs each day. When we couldn't find anything else to eat, we filled our stomachs by chewing on edible tree leaves. Our one set of clothing was getting thinner, with many tears and holes, but it still helped somewhat to keep us warm.

The day we raided the destroyed village and fled when we found the cache of machine guns and machetes, we'd also seen military uniforms. We had been tempted to steal them, but knew that would be a dead give away that someone had been there, and they'd come after us. I kept thinking of how much warmer our emaciated bodies would be if we'd sneak back and take some of the uniforms. I could perhaps find some more rice and dried meat, as well! I knew we could keep healthy and survive a little longer if we did! But the risk was too great!

We had been under the tall tree for a month when the weather changed. Rainy season had arrived! We'd had no real tools to use when building our hut, and were uncertain what would happen to it if we were caught in a big storm. We attempted to reinforce the roofing with tree branches, and the walls with wood scraps. A couple of days later, a rainstorm did arrive with strong winds.

Our shelter withstood and we didn't get wet! We were happy and proud of the job we'd done!

And then, what we feared all along took place – we had been discovered! In the darkness of the night, a loud voice demanded, "All the men who live in there must come out! The government needs you. If you do not obey, you will be taken to the highest authorities!"

I looked out, and despite the darkness, I could see soldiers, dressed in black and carrying guns, with machetes and ropes. It was plain that it wasn't our government that needed us, but the communists.

Sorn walked outside and I followed him. I asked the soldiers, "Where are you taking him?"

I saw a long line of men, both young and old, that had been captured already, standing at the edge of the nearby rice field. The soldiers shouted an announcement for all to hear: "It will be a long time before you women see your husbands, brothers and fathers. They will be put to work in the fields to produce rice, make ditches for irrigation, and will be trained to be soldiers who will move with our armies and do whatever work needs to be done at the front."

I knew, before he said this, that I might not see Sorn again. We had heard that most of the people taken to work in the fields never came back – but died from neglect, massacres or murder. Other wives, mothers, sisters and daughters had followed their men to this place, and I joined them as we watched our loved ones go until they finally faded from our sight. I felt that my whole body had lost its strength, but I was too frightened to slump to the ground. It was a very sad day when we saw our men march away single file, prisoners of the communists!

Early the next morning, the soldiers came for us. We were taken into a village to be added as slaves to the communists along with all the rest of the people in that village. Some women were to take care of the babies, young children and the elderly. Those of us with our own babies were put to work in the cafeteria. Those who were experienced with animals, would take care of the livestock: cows, pigs, goats, and chickens. Those who sewed would have to mend or make uniforms. Those who had backgrounds in farming were to make gardens. Surprisingly, the job of cleaning weapons fell to the women, also, in a place where the soldiers switched out their used weapons for clean ones when needed. There was a lady who was part of the communist team who took care of the medical supplies and the sick, and some were assigned to assist her.

I worked with five other women in the cafeteria. We not only prepared meals for the soldiers, but for the entire community. Before beginning our jobs, we were given the rules. "You must obey these rules to the letter," we were told. "You must let your men go. Do not try to sneak off to see them. If you or your men are caught running away, you will be killed. The punishment for escaping, is being burned alive."

I didn't know any of my co-workers – we were perfect strangers who would have to learn to work together. I was convinced the only way Kechara and I would survive was to do whatever they told me to do. The first days after Sorn was gone, I dedicated myself to adjusting to life in this communist community by making friends with the other women. I was told to help care for the toddlers, and when necessary to breastfeed other women's babies that were left in our care.

Little by little we ladies became acquainted. I quickly learned those who were trustworthy and those who were not safe to confide in. Any information we learned, we would share only with our secret and trustworthy friends.

Single women, widows, and teenagers were sent into the fields to work in the rice paddies. We were all from different towns and different backgrounds – some knew all about farming, while others were from cities. The soldiers kept the women segregated in groups. Old women helped in the cafeteria; but if they were too aged or infirm, they went into a primitive type of nursing facility.

Over time, the various groups bonded and leaned on each other. As a coping strategy, I pretended to be very happy while serving meals to the communists. I acted like I approved of them and found it a privilege to cooperate with them. Some of the women of the communist team were kind to everyone, but we still feared them.

Four weeks later we were regrouped, but those of us who had been working in the cafeteria kept meeting secretly; always encouraging one another to keep a low profile. We didn't want the communists to find any details out about our education or personal lives.

We were well aware that after taking over a country, the communist *cleansed it*! Their goal was to create a classless society, easy to be ruled, so their cleansing consisted of disposing of anyone who posed a threat. And the well-educated were considered a threat, which meant anyone found in that category would be killed. Therefore, I never shared with anyone that I could speak several languages, or that I had graduated from high school. All of us - my husband, my uncle, my cousin, my aunt and myself - were on the communist LIST of people to be killed, all because we were among those educated and could read and write Cambodian. Because of this we worked hard to hide our identities, we also had to pretend we were illiterate.

Killing was the communist way to success and there was a terrifying order to it: professionals and educated people were to be killed first, according to their doctrine, followed by the elderly. Old people were just in the way, and resources were wasted upon them. Their strategy included keeping younger people capable of hard work in the fields while disposing of the weak and old.

The women in our secret group discovered that many of the soldiers themselves, prior to communism, had been professors, doctors, nurses, college students and business owners, but they also hid this knowledge from the communist leaders – by acting as ignorant peasants, they were safer. The armed forces of communism are made up mostly of the ignorant and common people because they are more easily manipulated.

We knew right from the start that the communists had their own ways of learning the truth about those they captured. Anyone on the LIST was killed right from the start whenever the truth about them was discovered through the interrogation of other educated people, even though they promised they would not kill anyone who informed on others! Our cafeteria group was committed to remaining silent if asked about any of our members – claiming to not know much about each other.

In these situations, everyone is suspicious of everyone else. If you lied about yourself, and were found out, you were killed. So, you shared nothing, but just did your job. As a prisoner of the communists, I had no other choice but to serve them the best I could, and because I did, some of the leaders were kind to me and tried to build a relationship with me. I learned to show them respect, without letting down my guard. The younger soldiers had been trained to be indifferent to people – to kill without pity, and that is what they did, seemingly without conscience!

The teenage soldiers would show off with their machine guns, telling us they were going out into the jungles to shoot at targets. It was as though, now that they had joined the communists, they had cleared their minds of any of the love or mercy they'd ever been given; they quickly became incapable of demonstrating these qualities.

To keep Kechara and myself safe, I would play along with them, laughing with them and praising them for their skills in shooting.

They had no clue who I really was, other than just one of the Cambodian captives. I acted as if everything they did or said was important, which seemed to please them.

I became friendly with a communist leader who was female; she introduced herself to me as Kim. She oversaw the dispensing of medicine and the care of the elderly. For some reason, she trusted me right from the start, and began sharing things with me that I was sure were kept secret from the general population.

One day she asked quietly, "Would you like to take a walk? I'm going to show you where people are killed. It's a secret, and you must not tell anyone about it."

It was a long, long way from the village and the cafeteria where we'd become acquainted. When we reached the area where people were killed, the ground was splattered with blood. You could tell that bodies had been dismembered and their parts thrown here and there at the edge of a rice field, left to rot. I identified heads, arms, and legs, but some parts were unrecognizable. Along with the horrendous secret of how they were killed, was the horrible smell of rotting flesh and human guts – my stomach lurched and my heart was sad and broken.

Next, she led me to pit after pit where thousands of whole bodies had been thrown into these dumping holes. I felt ill, but since Kim retained control of her emotions, I tried to control mine and not reveal my shock. The massacre of thousands of innocent people from this and other villages, made me hate communism; indignation and anger rose up within me.

Our return walk was a silent one. She made no comments, and I somehow kept back the tears.

That night in my cabin, I could not sleep. Every time I closed my eyes, I saw the pits full of men, women, children, and babies piled one upon another.

I will never know just why this new friend had wanted to show me this! Secretly, did she want a witness to communism's cruelties? Did she regret her association with them? Could I trust her? Could she trust me? Was her motive to make me share my real self with her in return for her sharing such a secret with me – so that she could report me, and I would become a discarded body in a pit?

After a while, though, my misgivings left me, and I felt safe again with Kim. But I knew it was not wise to open up to her or share my life with her, even though she had a need to share hers with me! Despite my caution, I started to like her more and more, even though she was a communist.

Each day, I would teach Kim new things. She wanted to know how to cook and sew. In turn, she wanted to teach me about communism and all of its tricks and secrets. She taught me how to shoot guns and clean them. Sometimes we'd visit while cleaning guns and getting them ready for the soldiers. The most important thing that I gleaned from my time with Kim was how to please the communist leaders and keep on their good side.

I tried to find out where they kept the people they captured, but didn't come right out and ask her. As with the pits, however, I knew it was very secret, and if she wanted to, or had a need to, she would tell me on her own.

"The soldiers like to kill people at nightfall," Kim told me. "When you see soldiers walking captives away from the village, they will tell you they're going out for target practice; what they really were planning was to use the captives as their targets! Not many of the captured lived. It was easier to kill them than provide for them. The soldiers didn't mind killing people, and they sent slaves out

49

to dispose of the bodies. No one was allowed to know where the killings took place."

Kim made me promise not to let anyone know what I had seen, and I promised to keep it to myself.

I was put in charge of the cafeteria, and for the care of a few babies, including my precious Kechara. Whatever else I had to do, I never let her out of my sight! Many of the babies would get sick, and when that happened, my main goal was to keep her away from them, so she wouldn't catch what they had, even though I had to go on nursing them.

No two days were the same in the village. And I never stopped thinking about Sorn. He had been gone for quite some time and I was concerned about what had happened to him. I also constantly worried about my family in our village, and wondered if they had escaped to Thailand. I tried to find out if anyone knew my parents. I talked to villagers whenever I had the chance, but could find out nothing. I heard rumors that the people of my village, Sisophon, had been evacuated, or had all escaped to Thailand. I was very frustrated; I was so tired of keeping everything to myself, and wished I could talk freely once again, just to let someone know just how much I missed my family and my grandmother! But to even mention them could put them in danger.

It was a blessing for me and Kechara to be in the cafeteria where we had more to eat. She was almost a year old by then, and loved to be with me and to play with the other toddlers. Whenever my friend Kim saw her, she'd pick her up and hold her. Sometimes I would relax and forget that I was still being watched by the communist soldiers – and most likely, by her.

My relationship with the other women in the cafeteria was growing stronger. I felt loved and cared for. It felt good to share my cooking skills with them, and to tell them funny stories about my childhood that would make them laugh. During our short breaks from cooking, the laughter and teasing that went on, enabled us to forget for a brief time that we were prisoners.

We enjoyed cleaning up after meals, and our joy spread to others. Some of the elderly would come up to me and let me know how glad they were to have me in their village. I'd give them a little extra food, and help them to get their jobs done faster, making sure they got back to their cabins safely.

Some days in the cafeteria, when the soldiers seemed less angry and demanding, I relaxed just a bit with them, and would do some kind act to help them feel love and kindness. Perhaps if they are treated kindly, it will change how they feel about killing innocent people, I would tell myself. Every now and then, you'd see a soldier do something kind for a villager – and you'd remember that they were human after all.

One evening, my friend Kim, whispered in my ear, "You might be seeing your husband in a few weeks. The soldiers will be bringing that first crew back and taking a new team out to work on the irrigation project!"

That was good news! That night, I told my baby girl that she was going to see her father soon! She nodded her head and smiled as though she understood every word I said! And we played and played before falling asleep!

Kechara was starting to talk and had a few words she used consistently. I can't wait for Sorn to hear her. I can't wait to see him coming home, I kept saying to myself. A week went by, and I was still waiting! But I refused to give up hope. I hope he comes home healthy and that he can stay with me and our baby for a while! Maybe they will not send him away again.

And he came!

The sun was shining behind him as he walked toward our cabin. I didn't recognize him at first. He was very thin with a long beard and walked with a limp. When I realized who he was, I hoped he would still remember me and our baby daughter. But I needn't have worried!

He shouted our names and ran toward us with a big smile on his face. I just stood there stunned, holding the baby and looking at him! I'd never felt such joy in my life, as I did when I saw him coming. He was eager to tell me everything that had happened out in the rice fields.

"It was extremely hot, and some of the men took a short break to get out of the sun right after we got there, and were shot instantly," he told me. "I was very glad I hadn't joined them, and from then on I knew that to survive I would have to work very hard, and finish every assignment. Some days they made us work without food, but we were given water so we could keep going." We talked far into the night, and we cried at some things, marveled at others, and kept saying how much we'd missed each other.

Every day there were announcements from the communist team leader – some of these updates were good news, others, bad. The worst news of all was when we were told we were running low on food, and that they were going to limit food for everyone in the village. I was worried about Sorn, because he was so thin. I would steal food for him each day from the cafeteria so he could get healthy again.

"I am blessed to be working in the cafeteria," I told Sorn. "I get to keep our baby close to me and we have plenty of food to eat. I am responsible for some of the other babies in the camp, and breastfeed them, and have to eat a lot to keep my milk! Some of these precious babies I bring back to our cabin and put them to sleep with me at night, along with Kechara."

"Do you think the communists still have us on their LIST, and are they looking for us?" Sorn asked one day.

"I'm sure they do, and that is why we must keep on using fictitious names."

He worried about the time I spent away from the cafeteria, but I assured him I was okay. However, having seen the pits in the killing fields, I knew I shouldn't be too trusting or sure of myself, I needed to maintain a healthy fear. The communists were killing more men, women and children every day, not only here but everywhere in Cambodia! They wanted to stop us from producing any more children, and kept couples apart.

Though I had promised my friend Kim not to share what I'd seen, I found myself telling Sorn. He was shocked to hear about the killing fields, but more shocked that a communist leader had exposed me to such a secret!

"Manith, you must not tell anyone else. I'm very worried about your friendship and why she wanted you to know about this! Be very careful!"

"But she is truly a friend, Sorn. She comes to the cafeteria just to see me and Kechara. She picks our baby up and carries her about. You don't have anything to worry about," I assured him. But he was like my father, and warned me daily about associating with the communists!

One week later, a soldier came up to our cabin during the day and asked Sorn to take a walk with him to the rice field. My heart pounded! Neither of us knew what to say! Sorn knew he had to obey, and all I could think of were Kim's words when she told me: "When you see soldiers walking someone away from the village, they will tell you they're going out for target practice, but what's really happening is: they are about to use the person walking with them as the target!"

I watched Sorn and the soldier walking toward the rice field. I wondered if my husband would be coming back to me and little Kechara.

He came back that evening! "That soldier just needed my advice on how to build a small bridge at the end of one of the nearby lakes!" We sighed, and smiled in relief!

The same evening, Kim stopped by my cabin. "Your husband is at the cafeteria having dinner with my chief. I want you to come and join them."

Dinner had been prepared that day by some of the other women that were assigned to cafeteria duty. When the dinner was finished, both Sorn and I thanked our host, and then returned to our cabin, with many concerns in our hearts and questions in our minds! We had no idea why we had been so honored, and couldn't help but wonder if it was to throw us off and that soon we'd be marched off into the jungle. We whispered most of the night!

The next morning early, I went to the cafeteria to begin another day's work, and, as usual, I saw Kim coming in with a big smile on her face. She came over to me and let me know that her chief wanted us to build a cabin for ourselves next to his. As we had to do with any requests of the communist leaders, we agreed to move next to him.

That night we found ourselves whispering again. "Why do you suppose the communist leader and your friend Kim have befriended us?" Sorn asked.

"I have no idea. Maybe to keep an eye on us?"

"Do you suppose they've figured out who we are?" Sorn added before falling asleep.

The next day a few soldiers were assigned to help Sorn build the new cabin, and a week later we moved in, and our next-door neighbors were the Communist Chief and his family!

It was beginning to be clear to us, that the move wasn't necessarily just a friendly gesture, but probably it had been noted how hard a worker Sorn was, and the chief wanted him nearby as a sort of consultant. In a sense, it was a promotion from being a mistreated, expendable prisoner to being a useful person to the Communist cause – if you could call that a promotion!

Eventually, we were told they needed him to oversee the building of an irrigation system in a different district.

Sorn must say goodbye to his little daughter and to me once again. We hoped that he might be back in a couple of months. "I'm sure going to miss cuddling with Kechara, and those great big smiles she gives me! And you, Manith!" Sorn assured me.

Two months went by, and not a word from anyone about Sorn, or when he would be returning. I knew that if Kim found out anything, she would let me know. One day she told me that she wanted to talk to me, but it was very bad news for all of us in the village. Kim was in the first communist team to occupy our particular village, and now her group was being moved to a new location, and a new team would take over the village!

"I can't bring you and your family with me, but wish I could," she said. "The new team has more power and is higher up in the system – more rigid with their rules!"

I ventured to ask her a question, hoping I wasn't overstepping my bounds, "How many teams are there in Cambodia?"

"There are several teams and each one operates in a different way. Some have larger armies, and others just a couple of hundred soldiers," she answered, "But that is about all I know."

I had grown very close to Kim and she to me, and I almost broke down and cried when she told me I might never see her again.

"You will be okay, my friend. You'll remain in this village, and they will no doubt keep you on cafeteria duty. The new team will need a good cook, and I will recommend you!"

My friend Kim's team moved out, and the new team moved in. Kim had obviously kept her word, and I stayed on in the cafeteria as head cook for the new team. I was grateful to my friend, and kept hoping things would go just as well for us with this new change of guard.

There were more new babies to care for and many more soldiers to cook for. A few toddlers from the new team were also placed in my care. I was glad I had the same duties, but worried how things would turn out, working for the new team that was settling into the village.

Kim came by my cabin and gave me some wise counsel before she left. "We are never given notification that a change will take place, and have to be ready to leave whenever a new group arrives to replace us. So, my final advice to you is: think positively, be flexible – that's what I have been doing to survive. Work hard each day, serve well, and don't worry about tomorrow, because each tomorrow brings new challenges! You must be in good spirits and rested, ready for whatever comes your way. And one last thing: Do not trust anyone from the new group," she warned! "I have known you for six months, and you are a very friendly person – you will be a great benefit to any team, and I'm pretty sure they'll not want to get rid of you. But keep your distance and your own counsel!" She gave me one of her big smiles, turned and left. I knew that I hadn't been wrong to trust her, she'd turned out to be a good friend, one whose advice I would listen to.

A few of the women of the newly-arrived communist team, introduced themselves to me. They knew all about me, and seemed relieved to have someone trust-worthy living close to the cafeteria. It was convenient for them whenever they needed me. I was cooperative, and never refused them anything. I was determined to work hard, turn out well-presented food, keep my ears open, and my mouth closed.

Now that I lived near the cafeteria, I was able to keep tabs on what was going on in the village. I welcomed a couple more babies that were given into my care, and all things considered, I was kept busy and happy. Another month went by and I still didn't know when Sorn would return, or if he would come back!

The new group was harder to figure out. I heard some of the soldiers speaking Vietnamese – and this sounded a warning signal to me, knowing all the damage the communists had done in Vietnam. I didn't let anyone know that I understood the Vietnamese language, and heeding Kim's advice, I was careful not to be tricked by this more hardcore group of communists.

When the first group left, so did all the medicine - the new team brought none in with them. It was the same with food supplies, they brought nothing with them and depended on the Cambodian people of the village to provide for them. Some of the team members arrived ill with no medicine to give them - malaria, respiratory problems, and dysenteries were the main maladies. Besides so many being unhealthy, there weren't many young people – the majority of the soldiers were more mature, battle-weary adults and some were actually old. It seemed to me they were a much weaker bunch than the preceding team.

Some might be contagious, I thought, and spread their illnesses to the rest of the people in the village, including Kechara and myself! Not only would there be additions to the piles and piles of dead bodies in the pits of the killing fields, there could also be people dying right here in the village from diseases!

The leaders were very demanding and put a lot on the shoulders of the villagers, and the soldiers were just as ready to carry out punishments on the people!

They were not as organized as Kim's team, which ran as a well-oiled engine in comparison to how the new team worked. The changes came very quickly. The leadership was not as strong, and it was the younger members that rushed about making all the decisions. I could tell that the older, infirm communists received very little sympathy from the rash young soldiers who didn't seem to take orders from anyone, and were trigger-happy and cruel. Those that were near death when they arrived were assigned to the villagers who were expected to care for them, and bring them back to health – or else.

To survive, I told myself, I must do my job well, keep my distance and mind my own counsel, just as Kim advised!

Chapter Seven

A Guardian Angel Named Reep

About a month after the second team came, the aggression was such that we didn't know what to expect next – afraid at every turn. People were shot in the cafeteria while eating, without any provocation. *Taking someone's life means nothing to these communists,* I thought!

The stench from the open pits was terrible. They tried to burn the bodies, but there were so many of them, they wouldn't ignite. They threw old clothes, shoes and other debris into the pits to use as kindling, and when they started to burn, added dried vegetation and branches from trees to keep the fires going, but the bodies still wouldn't burn! I'll never forget the inescapable and intolerable odor. People would lose their appetites, vomit, and be sick!

Try as I would, it was impossible to free my mind from the assassinations, massacres, and terrible indifference of this heartless enemy that had captured us! And always present in my thinking were Kim's words: Don't trust anyone on the new team!

They came in among us with an animosity and rage that led to hundreds of killings from the first day they arrived, and it never stopped!

Two weeks later, yet another team moved into the village with several hundred more communist soldiers. As with the second team, they took command over the whole village, power-hungry and eager to kill! The anger on their faces was very intimidating.

The elderly were left to die in agonizing pain, totally ignored, which troubled me very much. I thought perhaps the brutalities of the former younger soldiers would not be as prevalent among the more mature soldiers on this team, but there was no difference!

As I went about my cafeteria duties, I sized up the new arrivals — and came to this conclusion: they are no improvement over the last — they're just as full of pride, anger and hate! They see us as enemies, though we have done nothing to oppose or harm them.

Whatever the team, they all seemed to despise weakness. If they saw vulnerability, they would push and kick people to demonstrate their power over them. And with those who were stronger, they'd initiate a fight, falsely-accuse the person, and end up killing him. The abuse of older people continued, and was really hard to see. They were beaten and kicked to death while living, their bodies treated with the same disrespect after death, thrown into pits to rot.

The younger soldiers found their fun in coming up to a captive who was eating and yanking away his food. They'd throw it on the ground, and force him to get down on his knees and eat it. If he refused, they'd walk away laughing, saying, "Oh, well, we'll soon be killing him anyway."

The younger soldiers were authorized to kill at will, treat people any way they wanted, and not required to give account to anyone for their crimes. The abuse got so bad that some of the villagers would run away in desperation and find caves to hide in, but few were successful in their attempts to escape. Most were found and killed.

And it wasn't uncommon for soldiers to throw the elderly and infirm into the pits alive. The holes had been dug so deep that it was impossible for them to climb to the top and escape. You could hear cries coming from inside the pits, begging for someone to come and rescue them.

One cruel communist team followed another, and the mistreatment never let up. They've been trained well to cleanse the land, by killing us! I would reflect.

I worried about myself. How will having witnessed these atrocities affect the rest of my life should I survive to tell my story? And who would have the courage to listen, if I should tell it? Who would believe that humans are capable of such cruelty?

The entire communist team, their families and little ones were fed together in the cafeteria, along with work crews made up of villagers – this way, more work could be accomplished. I made sure the soldiers were served first, and hoped they'd leave the premises before others were fed. The last to be fed were the elderly and children, who in our culture, should have been first!

I was always nervous when soldiers would stay around to watch the second round of people. I could feel them staring at me and would try to ignore them, but couldn't help but wonder what they were planning. On one occasion I heard a gun go off right outside the cafeteria! I looked to see what had happened. Two elderly men had been caught sneaking food, and they were lying on the ground dead! I thought, they've finally escaped successfully – they'll never fear or go hungry again!

What if I inadvertently did something to displease the soldiers who strutted around the cafeteria? Could I end up as their next target? Many times, after returning to my cabin after these stress-filled days in the cafeteria, I was sick to my stomach, and one night I suffered a nervous breakdown.

I slept, but in the morning, it felt like my muscles were paralyzed. I couldn't even rise from the bed! I couldn't move. I couldn't go to work, I just couldn't find it within me to prepare the food even if I'd have gotten there! I wondered if a person could die from exhaustion and shock. I lost my will to speak, and couldn't muster the energy to do anything but comfort Kechara.

I knew there were other women who could cook, but who would take care of the toddlers and infants – I was the one who breastfed them! Will someone cover for me, I wondered?

And while I was thinking about all of this, there was a knock on the door, and my heart stopped! I drug myself out of bed and tried to stand up, but couldn't. I crawled to the door. A middle-aged woman from the newest of the communist teams was standing there. I recognized her as the woman who lived in the cabin next to mine. "I've stopped by to check on you," I remember her saying.

She carried a small basket with soup made of rice and dried fish, and some hot tea. When I saw what she brought, I said, "How did you know I needed help?"

"When I asked why you hadn't shown up for work, I was told that you might be sick, because otherwise you would be there. I saw that there was no one to take care of the children, so I took care of them for you." She added, "One of the toddlers you've been taking care of is mine, and I appreciate your doing this while I'm in the rice fields."

When she told me that her husband was the new communist chief of the village, I felt very blessed by her friendliness. "I'm going to stay home for a couple of days," she told me, "and help you get back on your feet."

She told me her name, something all of us were hesitant to do! This convinced me that she was sincere in her concern for me. "My name is Reep," she said. Had I been a Christian at the time, I would have called her my guardian angel! It was wonderful to have someone show me kindness!

"Don't worry that you will get in trouble for being sick. Everyone gets sick now and then, including me! The soldiers will not do anything to hurt YOU! They like it that you serve them so well when they come in hungry to the cafeteria," she assured me. "Everyone likes you, because you're a good cook, and your meals are always on time. Even though supplies are short in the village, I'll try to bring you extra food so you can get well quickly. And I'll take care of your baby until you're better."

I thanked her, and Reep left.

No sooner had she gone, however, than I started to doubt. *One of the tricks of the communists, one of their evil ways to kill people, is to poison their food,* I told myself. *I'm not sure I should trust Reep! She might have poisoned this food!* I looked at the rice soup with dried fish – I felt the warm cup of tea. And before I knew it, I was eating and drinking and saying, *Well, if it poisons me, it poisons me – but at least I'll die with a full stomach!*

Before she left, I told her my name was Mahm, the fictitious name I had chosen for myself. I ate as much of the food as I could in my weakened condition, and saved the rest for the next day, all except what I fed Kechara! Reep had left saying, "Be sure you feed your baby!"

She became a good friend. She reminded me of Kim who'd left the village with the first team, but it took me longer to trust Reep than it had taken to trust Kim.

I woke up feeling better, and was soon back in the cafeteria cooking. But the uncertainty and fear that brought on my nervous breakdown remained - every time I heard gunshots I would tremble and grow weak! Though I had gained the respect of some of the communists, I never forgot that I was one of the many names on their LIST of people worthy of dying. They were hunting for people like me. I knew this because my education made me a threat to communism.

Chapter Eight

Thoughts of Escaping

There was no news from or about my husband Sorn! Since Kim, there was no one I could ask who might have information about where he was. I gave up hope of seeing him again. I just tried to live each day as it came – serving the communists who had snatched him out of my life!

Sometimes, I was tempted just to let the soldiers know who I was, that I was on their LIST so they could kill me and get it over with. But in my next breath, I would want to stay alive and find a way to escape from the killings.

Step one, I told myself, *stay your ground*. Step two, *learn all you can about each team*. Step three, *make appetizing meals to keep them dependent on you and serve them well*. Most importantly, step four, *when the opportunity to escape presents itself, don't hesitate – leave! For the time being, though, if I just perform the tactic described in step three to the best of my ability, there's less possibility I'll be suspected of planning to escape.*

I watched what they did, learned their 'tricks' and habits, and maintained my cautious friendship with Reep – all the while I waited for an opportunity to escape.

Reep began to let me know some of the secret plans of her team, and would let slip some of the things that were happening in other locations. She told me that when they captured someone whose name was on their LIST, they took the person to a different location to be interrogated, tortured, so they could get information concerning others on the LIST. If the person refused to cooperate, he was killed; if he did cooperate, he was still killed. The only thing he could gain by telling them the information they wanted, was that the torture might be stopped! This process was to be carried on until everyone on the LIST had met his/her doom.

The leaders favored using younger soldiers to kill and torture their victims, even when it was someone within their own ranks. Reep told me her husband, the chief of the team, confided to her that he wanted to kill off all the old communists as soon as they stopped being productive.

Many of the Cambodian young people volunteered to serve in the communist army. They believed the communists would be the winning army, so they joined it to survive and save their own lives – even when they had to volunteer information about family members who were on the LIST. When I was in high school, and the seeds of communism were first being introduced to us students, I knew many teenage boys and girls who, under obligatory school programs, learned to use firearms. I saw how quickly they became hardened as I witnessed their displays of anger when they'd miss their targets.

It was sad for me to see how quickly some of our own people became traitors, and learned to be fierce, cruel and unfeeling – killing people as though they were hunting animals in the fields and jungles! They learned to give orders, even to those older than themselves who they had been brought up to respect. With a sense of pride, they upheld the rules and regulations of communism!

Indoctrination is a very strong thing, and a vital tool of communism.

There was no village in Cambodia where people were not dying at their hands. As our people were being killed, our culture died with them! Respect and veneration of old people was the golden rule of Cambodian culture, and before my very eyes, I beheld its demise!

When I observed Cambodian young people, turned communist soldiers, mistreating and killing the elderly, I asked myself: What kind of family ties do these soldiers have? Do they have grandparents? Or are they orphans who have embraced communism as a sort of parent whose evil orders they willingly obey?

Everyday, I passed by the places people were led to be killed, either in the rice fields or at the edges of the village. I longed for a day when the pits, the deep holes and the untidy graves of innocent people, would be a thing of the past! Whenever I would come upon a pit, I would look with terror to see if I could recognize any of the members of my own family among the dead bodies that were visible.

One of the main reasons people were killed was for stealing food. Sometimes they were shot on the spot, and their bodies would lie in a corner of the cafeteria where I worked until someone finally came to drag them out to the killing fields. Other times they'd be apprehended at night while sneaking into the cafeteria, and be marched out to the pits. It was not at all unusual to go to bed, and hear women crying and begging for forgiveness before a gun would be fired. And we'd know that another hungry person had lost her life – while a soldier had another notch on his gun and on his conscience!

Every week, the communists would gather everyone in the village and count them. All of the men would be sent to work in the fields farthest away. If someone tried to escape or fight back for any reason, they were killed openly.

One night as I was walking through a wooded area toward my cabin I heard a sound coming from behind a large tree of someone being whipped. I hid myself and tried to see what was happening. A young soldier was mercilessly whipping an older man who alternately pleaded for mercy and screamed for help. I could hear him clearly saying over and over again: "Don't kill me!" And then silence. The soldier turned on his flashlight, and I could make out that he was slashing and cutting the body of his victim.

I turned, and ran back to my cabin, shaking with fear, having witnessed a soldier stabbing someone to death. The next morning, I wondered about who it might be and if he could still be alive.

I went to work in the cafeteria as usual, but after a while, I told the other women I was going to the garden for some vegetables. On my way, I walked in the direction of the large tree, and looked behind it. I saw a dead body, and beside it, a discarded, bloodied machete. I walked closer, and I recognized the person's face. It was my uncle who I loved dearly and respected. He was a medical doctor, and had been on staff at a hospital in the capital city of Phnom Penh. I knew that my uncle had been wanted by the communists for quite some time – well, they had found him!

Earlier Reep showed me a LIST of the fugitives who were being hunted down, I acted as though I recognized none of them. But I had seen my own name, my husband's, my uncle's, one of my aunt's, and my cousin's on that horrible LIST. And here I was, looking down at my uncle whose death I'd witnessed the night before, and could do nothing to help him! Despite my shock and sorrow, I couldn't cry, for if I did, the communists would find out who I was. I knew they were still searching for people like Sorn who had worked for the government, and for doctors like my uncle, and for students like my auntie and myself, and for police officers like my cousin!

The search was still on, and I knew the communists would never give up looking for us. Reep did not know my real name, nor did anyone – people saw me, but my identity remained hidden.

Reep trusted me, and I trusted her, but I didn't tell her my real name. I made sure that, even if they tortured her, she'd be unable to give them my name. I didn't know how they'd found out who my uncle was, but they did. And I knew that in time, if I stayed in the village, someone would recognize me. And when that happened, they would not just kill me, but Kechara as well!

The next day, I went back to see if my uncle's body was still there. It was! I took another good look at him. Both of his arms had been tied behind his back, his head was severed from his body. His chest had been cut wide open and stuffed with dead grass. I sobbed. I was angry with the communist soldier who did this to him, and wanted revenge. His face had become almost unrecognizable, but I knew it was him. My anger turned to rage; I wanted to find the soldier and kill him.

I asked myself: *Why did I never see my uncle in the village or the cafeteria? Where did he hide, and how did they find him?*

Then I remembered Reep telling me that when they captured a person, that person was used as a tool to find other people on the LIST. Enough torture – and people would break down, and tell what they knew! Could the soldier have been interrogating my uncle, and my uncle refused to inform on others in our family?

My throat and chest hurt all day, like it does when you have to hold back your tears instead of allowing the sobs to come. I wished that I could ask Reep if she had heard about any students or government workers that had been captured recently by the communists, but was too afraid to broach the subject. I knew though, that if I did ask her, she would always tell me the truth.

I kept telling myself: I must move through one day at a time, and keep on pretending innocence, and that I didn't know anything about anybody. I was well aware that it was only a matter of time when I would be found out, and captured. I had to get away before that happened!

One day we were told to gather at the river bank for an announcement.

This time, it was more like an object lesson than a mere announcement! Standing among others, I looked farther down river, and at a distance, thought I saw bodies floating. Before us, lined on the edge of the river, stood five men. Their hands were tied with rope and heavy chains. Their heads were covered with black plastic bags; their faces could not be identified.

Why are they calling us all together to witness what they're about to do? What came to my mind was that it was yet another trick of the communists, a scare-tactic to make us admit our true identities.

The announcement began: "We want you to know that this is one of the punishments we have for those who withhold information from us." I had been right! And they proceeded with the 'object lesson!'

They cut off the hands of two of their victims, and slashed their bodies before throwing them into the river. The victims, of course, would die by drowning if they didn't bleed to death first. The soldier did not pull the black plastic bag from the first four victims. But when they did pull the bag off the last, I saw that it was my cousin!

Those of us gathered gasped as each one fell into the water. When I saw my cousin's body slashed and cruelly pushed into the river, I collapsed on Reep and fainted!

When I came too, the communists had taken me to one side and were waiting to interrogate me.

"What made you faint?" one of the interrogators asked.

"I was not feeling well, and had not eaten any food before we were told to come to the river bank," I answered.

Reep spoke up, "I can take her back to her cabin."

That was after they asked, "Did you recognize the person from whom the black bag was removed?"

Before answering, I thought about how I'd discovered my uncle beheaded, and I knew: someone has given information about my family members who are on the LIST, who of us will be next? Quietly I said, "Yes, I did. He was my cousin."

I knew that nothing I said or didn't say could save him now, for his body had joined the others, and he was floating down the river – set free. But I was not free – I could be the new next!

Among thousands of other innocent people, two of my family members had now been killed! I wanted so badly to let my parents and grandmother know about them. But I didn't know where my family was.

I was let go, and Reep took me home.

When I saw her crying the next day, I asked if she was okay. She looked around to determine we were not being watched and that what she was about to say could not be heard. She said, "One of the five, was my brother."

We encouraged each other to be strong and to let our loved ones go.

Reep told me that what had made her brother a threat to communism was his work - her brother had been a police officer in a large city. I wanted to tell her that my cousin had been a policeman too, but not even to her would I confess that! Between our friendship stood the awful truth that Reep was a communist and I was not!

I heard loud crying and screamed coming from the village. It was the high chief's wife. I could tell from the way she cried that she was mourning his death. He had been murdered on the same night that my cousin and Kim's brother had been killed. I was so confused and had hundreds of unanswerable questions and said to myself, *why would anyone murder the highest chief of this team of communists?*

Four soldiers carried his body away from the village. I went to let Reep know right away. We ran to our cabins, and tried to stay calm. The reason for his death was a mystery, but it was a well-known-fact, no matter who you were, if orders came from the top leadership, you would be killed. The names of those at the top were kept unknown!

Reep and I continued our close friendship. She opened up to me, more than I did to her. She told me her life story and all about her family. She loved my baby and there was no doubt in my mind about how much she cared for me. I was surprised, though, when she confided, "I will escape from the third team one of these days. My husband is already in hiding!" I believed her, and I wanted to let her know that I would escape one day, too, but kept this to myself.

A week after the chief's body was carried out, a new chief came to replace him.

Chapter Nine

Kachara's Grave

L iving conditions in the village were getting worse. More and more people were starting to get sick. It hadn't rained for many months and the land was so dry that the rice crops were dying. Young children and the elderly were the sickest. Daily, some would die from malaria and fevers. The extreme hot weather didn't help! When we dished up food, the plate would quickly be covered with mosquitoes and flies. One had to eat with one hand while shooing away the insects with the other. It was hard to eat with the smell of death ever present, and knowing that the insects came from the nearby pits.

I remember when my baby girl started to get sick. The first symptom was diarrhea, which lasted many days. I was concerned, and asked Reep for medicine. It helped, and after a couple of days it stopped. Not a week later, however, she stopped eating. She cried and I knew it was the awful headache one gets when you have malaria. I held her close and whispered in her little ear, "I love you, little one, my little Kechara!"

She began to refuse food, and never regained her appetite. Some nights she slept, and other times she cried all night long. I became exhausted. I tried everything I could think of to bring her back to health. Nothing worked!

Kechara had been sick for over two weeks, when I asked Reep for more medicine.

"We hardly have any malaria medicine left," she told me, "and what we have, I don't have access to. A soldier put a lock on the door where the supplies are kept, and I don't have a key! I won't be able to help you get medicine any longer."

Kechara worsened and became very thin. She cried less, and looked so helpless just lying there, looking up at me with big, sad eyes. She couldn't walk, and would fall backward if I tried to set her up. She began to refuse my breasts. I tried to give her water, but she couldn't keep it down. Two months had passed since my baby first got sick. Now, she lay there quietly, never moving other than the breaths she took.

If she did look at me, it was with a look of profound sadness – had she been older and understood about death, I'm sure she would have told me she was ready to die. But, I did know about death, and I was not ready to let her go. I watched as her breathing slowed, and two days later, in the middle of the night, my baby girl gently breathed her last breath and was gone.

When I discovered it, I held her tightly to my chest and cried very hard. I felt empty. I was totally alone now! I had always counted on having my precious child with me always, but she was gone. I fell asleep, and when morning came I was still cradling Kechara in my arms and I didn't want to let her go!

Communism had robbed me of the medicine and medical help that could have saved her! What a hopeless existence was ours. The next day, Reep came with some news that added to my sadness. She told me, "There was someone from your village that was here briefly and asked me to let you know that your 104-year-old grandmother has passed away from poverty!"

I would not see my grandmother again! Unthinkable! I longed for another family member to mourn with me – but there was no one. I thought my family had escaped to Thailand. But, evidently not, for she had died in our village.

I got up and started to dig a grave for Kechara in the dirt floor of my cabin. I was so sad, I talked to myself – I just had to talk with someone! I repurposed a container I had, I made it into a cozy little coffin. When I slipped Kechara's tired little body into it, I said over and over, "I'm so sorry, my baby, that I couldn't save you. I tried to keep you alive, but, you see, they would give me nothing to take away your sickness. I wish I could have taken you to a doctor. But you will meet your great uncle and your great grandmother – and they will take care of you."

I lay next to her grave every night when I went to sleep, so she would not feel all alone. Kechara meant 'first child,' and I loved her in a very special way. I stayed in the cabin with my baby's grave and did not go back to the cafeteria to cook for the soldiers for about a week.

Reep would come to check on me, to see if I needed anything. She told me that the communists now had a new team leader. "They will make the announcement soon to the whole village. It's important you do not stay away from the cafeteria for too long. The soldiers are already asking about you. Most of the elderly are too."

I must take courage, as Reep advised, and get back to work in the cafeteria, I told myself. I worked each day, but could hardly wait to get back to my baby's grave each night! Being close to her was my only comfort.

Food and medical supplies were getting dangerously low in the village. We were also running out of salt, rice, beans and meat, our main staples. Disease and sickness increased from lack of food.

Strokes, diabetes and lung diseases were main causes of death, as well as malaria that never let up.

We were informed that the third team would be moving out in a couple of days, and a fourth communist team moving in!

More babies and small children were getting symptoms similar to those that had taken Kechara's life – diarrhea and high fevers. And when the new team came, with them a new brand of sickness that spread throughout the village.

The elderly and children were dying from malaria. I watched as the soldiers would snatch babies out of their mothers' arms as soon as they died. Their mothers begged to bury them, but instead, they were tossed into pits full of rotting corpses. The grieving parents would be ordered back to work in the fields.

Reep caught me crying in the cafeteria, and had to remind me to try harder to let my baby go. I appreciated her comfort and counsel. She encouraged me to be strong and not let the soldiers see my emotions. "Don't expect any sympathy from the fourth team. They don't really care who dies. To them it's just one less mouth to feed!" she told me.

One evening, Reep stopped by to see me, but this time with good news. "I have found out where your husband has been taken," she began. "He was in hiding with other former communist team members near the border of Thailand when they found him," she said.

"He's still alive! What a relief!" I told her. "I want to escape and go to him; I'm desperate to see him so I can tell him about Kechara. And if I die, I want to die with him!"

"That's dangerous thinking," she told me.

I went to work at the cafeteria as usual, did my work as efficiently as always, but was secretly searching for a way to escape.

I heard a sudden shout for joy one day from the soldiers! They were talking loudly and telling each other that tomorrow night would be special!

"They've captured and rounded up lots of students and government workers and are bringing them here to be burned. The whole village will be as bright as if we had electricity," they shouted!

"They're going to select one of the younger soldiers," they said. "And he will be the honored one who gets to set them afire!"

Reep quietly told me, "This is the diversion we need! While the team is engaged in burning their victims, we can escape from the village."

But the next night, when it was time for us to leave the cafeteria, we saw some of the women they had captured being tied up with ropes. They were crying, and begging for mercy. We heard one of them say, "Please let me go, let me live, I will serve the community for the rest of my life!"

Others were braver, standing up to their captors, and shouting, "You deceived us and we fell for it! You told us we'd be safe if we did what you told us to do, and it was all a lie!"

The soldier started kicking them and yelling, "SHUT UP!"

As they got nearer to the cafeteria, where we were, I recognized my Aunty!

I had not seen her since before I was captured. I wanted to run to her and hug her, but had to pretend I didn't know her. It had been discovered that she was a nurse, and had been taken by force and was now going to die – too intelligent to let live, a threat to communism. You'd think they'd have let the doctors and nurses live to help with the sickness, their own included, but communism is not a rational dogma.

The soldier shot seven women, one right after another. His fellow soldiers helped to throw them into the fire pit, which had become a roaring flame. It went on and on: killing, and tossing bodies into the flames. More wood tossed in when needed to keep the fire at a roaring pitch. The horrible smell of human flesh burning made me want to run away. I was sobbing, and Reep whispered a warning, "Stop it! Don't display your emotions or give any sign to the soldiers that you are grieving!"

I obeyed, even though one of the women they shot was my aunt.

The new chief came into the cafeteria and spoke to us: "Make some special food! We want to make this a great celebration for the soldiers who are participating in this ceremony of lights!"

Our well-laid plans were ruined because of the chief's request! Controlling our anger and our disappointment, we started making food worthy of this new, great accomplishment – the massacre of some special women, students, and professionals!

I lay down that night next to our baby's grave and cried. I kept seeing her face, my uncle's, my cousin's and my aunt's. I knew they had all died, but I couldn't let go of any of them! I dreamed about them, but most of my dreams were about my daughter. Sometimes they were so real, I'd wake up and think she was still alive and playing around me.

Her sweet little voice would wake me up in the middle of the night, calling out, it seemed, from the grave! I actually heard her and felt the familiar weight of her little body in my arms! She was always wearing the little pink dress I made for her, which was her favorite. And I would see her lying sweetly covered with her blanket in her coffin!

I thought about her favorite blanket, and how we had found it lying on the ground at the border of the rice field. She had claimed it as her own as soon as she saw it! Fish and rice were her favorite foods. She loved to eat soft, sweet mangos and oranges. The memories I have of her remain in my heart to this very day – how she died, and how I would lay down beside her grave to go to sleep with memories too precious to let go of.

Another thing that haunted me at night was the vision of new-born babies being torn into four pieces by soldiers as their mothers watched, soon after giving birth – and then, before they could weep for their poor babies, the soldiers would shoot the mothers.

These senseless atrocities were happening in all of Cambodia's little villages!

Reep and I decided to stay put in the village for a couple more days or weeks until another diversion would occur and we could slip away.

The soldiers continued their torture of the elderly who they considered a senseless drain on the food supplies. They would cut off their fingers and toes and leave them to bleed to death, or pull the nails from their fingers; some died from shock and pain, and others lingered to be tortured on another day. The soldiers' only reaction to what they'd just inflicted was to laugh as they walked away. It is hard to put into words to make others comprehend just how lost, terrified, sorrowful and helpless one feels when witnessing these kinds of things daily, knowing there was absolutely nothing that could be done to help or prevent it!

I saw Reep running to me, out of breath and saying, "We have to leave before nightfall!" The expression on her face really concerned me.

"Tell me, why do we have to leave so soon?"

"They're planning to kill everyone in the village, men, women, children, babies and the elderly – if we don't leave we're all going to die tonight!"

"They say it's to get rid of the diseases!" she explained. "The bodies will be burned along with everything else in the village! Some of the soldiers are against it, but the leaders have been given orders to do this. They're in disagreement and are fighting among themselves over this drastic order from the 'top authorities.'

Reep started gathering all the food she could find, and I packed some rice. I looked then at Kechara's little grave and told her, "I can't just abandon her grave! I will not leave her alone in the cabin! I'll stay here and die with her."

"If you decide to do that, you can, but you will be burned alive with the rest of the village!"

She told me this was the last possible opportunity we'd have to escape. The soldiers had been ordered to leave before sunset for an important, secret meeting outside the village. And when they returned they would find the whole village burning. They've been told that all must attend the meeting and no one is allowed to be missing; there will be a mass murdering of the unsuspecting villagers.

The past year had been a combination of survival and tremendous loss! I had lost my sweet grandmother, an uncle, an aunt, a cousin, my precious first child, and was also separated from my husband, not knowing if he was dead or alive. I had witnessed the deaths of hundreds of innocent people across all ages, and seen the pits full of the many thousands who perished in the killing fields! Now, my time was running out, and I had only one option left if I were to survive – escape!

Reep and I must leave before the soldiers returned from their 'meeting.' Reep needed to find out where her husband was hiding, and I must locate Kechara's father. I was still hoping to find him where I last learned he was hiding, with other escapees near the Thailand border. I desperately needed to tell him that our little daughter had died.

We watched as the soldiers marched out of the village. We started to make our move as soon as we were sure they were gone. The village felt haunted by all the atrocities experienced at the hands of the various teams – and Reep and I were anxious to be on our way!

We were escaping together, but our journeys would be different, so Reep and I said our last goodbyes with tears; she gave me a bag of cooked rice with dried meat which she'd wrapped in banana leaves. I gave her a jug of water and some ripe bananas.

"I'll never forget the comfort and help you were when Kechara was so sick, and for the medicine you risked bringing me! And for being with me when she died!" I told her.

"Cooking and preparing meals with you, forgetting that I was one of the team, and you a prisoner, was so much fun! We're going to miss all the small, innocent children and babies that we cared for, won't we?" were her parting words.

I left the village after Reep did. I had to say goodbye to Kechara. With a broken heart, I walked into my cabin for the last time. I sat in the dark alone beside my baby's grave. I cried very hard, and whispered, "Dearest Kechara, I don't want to leave you alone, but I must go to find your father." I stood up bravely then, and left. I kept stopping and looking back until I could no longer see the cabin that sheltered Kechara's resting place. I wanted to turn around one more time, but the fear of being caught by the soldiers, hurried me along.

I never forgot my baby; as long as I live, she'll remain in my heart!

With every step I took, Reep's words kept echoing in my mind: keep walking through the night, and do not stop to rest!

I was fleeing as fast as I could go, and in my imagination I could see Kechara alive and well, sitting in front of the cabin, smiling, waving, and calling, "Goodbye, Mahrk (Mother)!" It was so real, I almost turned around and ran back to grab her up and bring her with me!

I was brought back to reality, however, when my right foot got stuck in the mud of a rice field and my leg went in up to my knees. I felt something piercing the bottom of my foot. With effort, I managed to pull my foot free of the mud, and was startled to see that I had stepped on a long, corroded nail attached to a piece of wood!

I couldn't go on until I pulled the nail out, and when I did, blood gushed out! I kept walking, but the pain was severe, and soon my leg hurt clear up to my knee. I was forced to stop walking when I came to the edge of the rice field.

As I sat there, resting my foot, I let my imagination loose again, and my baby's big smile, the one her Papa had said he'd miss when he left us, comforted me – and soon I had the courage to continue on despite the pain, saying, "Goodbye, my Kechara, this will be our last goodbye. I must stop dreaming, and keep going forward; and you must let me go! I need to get as far from the village tonight as I can, so the soldiers won't find me!"

And then, I said, "Lead me to your papa, and give your *mahrk* peace in her heart!"

The night was black when I took off once again, I couldn't see where I was walking, nor in which direction I was going. Yet, new energy flooded through me; I felt my baby girl's guidance and was sure I was going in the right direction, and that I would be safe! I judged my distances by how much farther I was from the cabin – from her little grave. Once, I stumbled, and realized I had fallen on top of some of the dead bodies that had been left to rot in the rice fields.

The moon came up, and it seemed to be intentionally looking down on me, and I could now see a little better to navigate the watery, muddy, dangerous rice fields. The dead bodies I came upon didn't frighten me at all, and I showed them the respect they deserved. I felt calmer now that I could see better, and I tried not to think about Kechara. I grew hungry and stopped briefly to eat some rice, and then took off again, and at times I would wonder how Reep was doing, hoping she had found her husband.

I walked the entire night, overwhelmed by the sadness and sorrow that would come and go within me.

The sun started coming up in the east, and was soon shining brightly overhead. I reached into my shirt pocket, to make sure I still had the letter that Reep and I had written in case we got stopped by soldiers on the road. It went more or less like this: To whom it may concern, this woman has my permission to travel to (a made-up destination). The signature was that of an (also made-up) communist official.

I took out some beef jerky from the other side of my pocket, and ate it as I walked. From far away, I heard the sound of automobiles. I had come to a road used by motorcycles, military trucks, and other vehicles. I hoped one of them would stop and give me a ride. By this time my injured foot was giving me a lot of trouble. I found a long stick to use as a crutch, and managed to leave the rice field that had been difficult and dangerous to navigate, and, walking on the road was kinder on my foot. Everywhere I stepped, I left a bloody footprint behind. I saw a dirty plastic bag alongside the road, and used it to wrap the wound to keep the dirt out.

Finally, I sat down at the side of the busy road to rest my foot. I was familiar with the highway and knew that it led to the border between Cambodia and Thailand! I hoped it would lead me to where Sorn was. When I tried to stand, the pain was excruciating. And I had to sit down again, wondering what to do.

About then, a motorcycle with two soldiers passed me. About the time I was going to say, *whew!*, it turned around and pulled up where I was sitting. I wondered if I would need the letter, and took it out of my pocket. One of the soldiers got off the motorcycle and walked toward me.

"What are you doing, and where are you going?" he asked.

My voice shook with fear as I answered, "I'm going to visit my family."

I showed him the letter. I knew that most of the soldiers did not know how to read or write, and hoped he was one of them! I stayed quiet and waited for him to speak. By this time the other soldier had come over, and he showed the letter to him, saying "Can you tell if she is telling the truth? She claims it's a letter with permission to travel."

Without answering him, the other soldier just stood there, looking at me. "What's your name," he asked.

"My name is Mahm." (Using, of course, the name I'd chosen to hide my identity.)

He smiled. And without a word, he pulled out a paper from his pants' pocket. On it was printed the picture of a woman. He showed it to me and asked, "Do you know who this is?"

I looked at the picture. It was me! I shook my head, and said, "No, I don't know who she is."

One of them said, "It's a well-known fact that there are look-alikes, but it's clear to see she's not the good-looking person in the picture!"

They searched my bag, patted me down and made sure there was nothing I was hiding. They couldn't have helped but notice that my foot was bleeding, but they offered me no help. They were soon on their way, and I was still free! And I finally indulged in a very relieved *whew!*

I stood on the side of the road and waited for a truck to come by, hoping to get a ride to the next town.

Now I knew, because of the picture they'd showed me, that my escape had been discovered, and that my picture was being circulated as someone who was wanted!

What I had learned from living so many months with the communists, was that their teams were made up of soldiers without a country, with nothing of their own – no land, no life, and no feelings! To fulfill their mission, the foot soldiers were pawns in their leader's hands. They did all the dirty work, accumulated cruelties on their own consciences, while the blood on their leaders' hands could only be seen by God. I knew that unless Cambodia had help, the pits in the killing fields would continue filling up with the bodies of innocent people and their children!

I sat on the edge of the road with my mixed-up thoughts and a very aching foot, feeling lost and empty. I felt so lonely. I didn't know where the soldiers had taken Sorn, and knew nothing about my parents or my brothers and sisters.

I thought, *if I ever reconnect with my family we'll once again lean on each other and face things together – then it won't matter if I live or die!*

I got up, finally, and started walking very slowly. I managed to reach the next town, which was called Mongkol Borey. Because the villages were very close to each other, this town was close to Sisophon, my home town. Mongkol Borey was under communist rule, of course. In order to rest my foot, though, I decided I would have to put myself under a communist team again.

(I have lost track of how many teams I lived with, but, this was probably the fifth!)

Chapter Ten

Reunited with Sorn

I blended in with the Mongkol Borey community, and as far as they knew, I was joining the communists of my own volition! For a good two months I worked in the cafeteria, as a cook. I found out that this team was different from the other teams. Though they were less cruel in many ways, they continued their diligent hunt for the people on the LIST. Whenever the soldiers patrolled an area, I would go into the deeply wooded places to hide, because my name was on the LIST, and my picture was circulating as a person of interest! Keeping a low profile, staying away from crowds, not getting too friendly with anyone, was now more important than ever!

The saying, 'If you can't beat them, join them,' became the Cambodian villager's mantra of survival! In essence, though we deplored the killings and cruelties, we were forced to blend in with their schemes, if we wanted to survive! Within a 'team' were work teams, made up of people who did the grunt work, teams of soldiers who did the 'search and kill' operations, and the lackeys who dragged the people they killed to the pits to dispose of their bodies! As for the leaders, they received their orders from headquarters, and carried them out to the letter!

Newcomers to a village were careful about what they said, and no one, but the communists, asked them questions! Whether a new arrival, or whether someone had been there for a while, no one offered information about themselves.

There were about three hundred soldiers on this team. They would march the work teams out to the farthest areas, and were told to kill any of the work team that couldn't keep up. New pits were dug, and when they became full, a 'mop-up-team' would attempt to cover the deep, communal grave, but many of the pits were left open!

The leaders, and the work teams would have wives and children with them. Medical supplies and medicines were always in short supply, and doctors rarely available. This affected the health of children especially. With no proper hygiene or clean water to drink, everyone was affected in some way. Many continued to die of malaria. And many were dumped in the rivers when they refused to inform on their friends and loved ones. Our only source of drinking water was the contaminated river; we had no choice but to drink water from rivers polluted by the dead bodies floating in it!

One of the tactics of the communist leaders was to limit the food for people on the work teams, and to then make them work even harder. Here in this new village, where I was not known, I became just another expendable person, and I had to work day and night. Sometimes I would become so exhausted and hungry that I'd pass out.

To fill our stomachs while working in the rice fields, we would chew on tree leaves to make it through the day, along with catching small insects, crickets, frogs and rabbits for protein! Whenever we found these kinds of things we'd share them with each other. This type of diet, however, if it is followed for too long, will irritate the stomach. This happened to me, and I became very sick with diarrhea. Mothers would even have to feed these things to their babies when their breast milk would diminish from such poor nutrition, and the small babies suffered from constant diarrhea.

The sight of skinny babies, with eyes that seemed bigger than their heads, would make my arms ache to hold and comfort them as I had Kechara when she looked at me so mournfully! I would recall how I had shared my breast milk with the babies of mothers on work teams, and with some of the leader's babies; and how I'd loved each one of them as my own.

Working in the rice fields was very hard on me. When the communist team let it be known they needed cooks, I applied, and once again worked in the kitchen, a job I enjoyed. It was challenging, though. Not only did I serve food to the soldiers and others who worked in the village, I had to prepare food to send out to the men who worked in the farthest rice fields. The kitchen crew was also responsible for the care of team member's babies day and night; when I would babysit them, it would comfort me, but, at the same time, make me miss my sweet Kechara.

When there wasn't enough water for everyone, the soldiers would kill some of the people by beheading them – it never became less frightening to see this happening.

I kept hoping that Sorn would show up on one of the work teams. I kept asking people about him, and one day I was told that he was very ill with an infectious disease, and had been quarantined him away from the people, so it wouldn't spread among them.

Day after day I would search for him, and one day I found him. He was lying on a very dirty wicker mat, all alone and in pain. He was moaning – and semiconscious.

I came to the door and tried to talk to him. I wanted him to know that I was there and wanted to take care of him. He recognized my voice and weakly responded, "Don't come any closer! This disease is very contagious, that's why the communists have isolated me, and have left me to die." He told me he hadn't had anything to eat for weeks!

I went to the chief and begged him to let me take Sorn to a doctor across the border in Thailand. "If he doesn't get medical help, he's going to die," I told him.

"I can't let you do that," he said, "It would be less complicated for you to just let him die. You must produce rice and cook meals if you want to survive, yourself! Forget your husband!" And with that cruel statement it was the end of our conversation.

Without another word, I decided to move into the quarantine cabin with Sorn, and if I caught the disease, I would lie down and die with him.

I feared I might be missed in the rice fields and in the kitchen, but no one reported me, and I did my best to take care of Sorn, even though it meant I would have to find a way to steal medicine and food. Some days I turned up for work at the kitchen, and let them think I was in the rice fields on the days that I didn't show up to cook! I told myself: *I will not lose one more person, especially my husband who now means more to me than anyone else!*

I let Sorn know about Kechara, and the killings of my uncle, aunt, and cousin. We would talk about them, and miss them together. I kept wondering how Kim and Reep were, and told Sorn how much they had helped me. I had grown hardened toward the communist soldiers, though, refusing to live in fear of them! I would remind myself of the saying – Fear is all in one's mind. Because the soldiers seemed more prone to kill the fearful and helpless, I was determined to remain strong.

No matter how dangerous Sorn's disease was, no matter how much he wanted to keep me from getting it, I had promised myself to take care of him, and I would do it! I was <u>not</u> going to have him taken away from me again.

"Since Kechara's death," I told Sorn, "I have become more protective of what belongs to me – letting other things go." I knew, however, that to stay out of trouble, I needed to work some of the time. So, when a woman on the kitchen crew would come for me, I would go to the kitchen with her and help with the cooking. But, at night, I would hurry back to my husband!

We will all die when it's our turn, but as long as Sorn is alive, I'll fight to keep him alive, I kept telling myself. Probably, the guilt feelings I had about Kechara's death, made me more determined than ever to prevent his.

Though at first I'd thought this team less cruel, eventually they showed their true colors. I started to see and hear about more and more killings. Not just at gunpoint, but horror stories of what seemed to be killing for the fun of it! As in the other village, the smell of the dead bodies soon became oppressive. The odor of the water we drank, coming from rivers and lakes, gave evidence to the increasing number of dead bodies floating there.

I told Sorn that when our baby passed away a soldier came to the house and told me to get rid of her body! They insisted I leave her dead body in the jungle for the animals and elements, and told me I needed to get back to work with the rest of the women in the cafeteria. They told me I'd had enough time off.

"What did you do when they told you that?" he asked.

"I was so angry with the soldiers, I ended up fighting back with words that I should not have said! I told them to go ahead and kill me so I could be with my baby again! I felt so much hate! You'd think they'd have had some pity when a little child died, but it was nothing to them – there was no mercy shown at all," I vented. "And when my family members were killed, I wanted revenge."

One day I heard gunshots and knew that someone in the rice field had just been killed. We became very serious, and knew very well, if we didn't get away, it would be our turn to be targets for the heartless soldiers to practice on!

I hadn't learned yet the name of the dreaded disease that Sorn had. Then, one day we heard a woman's voice calling to us. We were still asleep when she and her husband came to wake us up. I went to the door and found an elderly man and woman, Mr. and Mrs. Cong. After her initial greeting, the woman said, "It is time to wake up!"

They had brought food and drink for us. And as the elderly do, they had much wisdom to impart, and their words gave us inner strength.

"Our son had leprosy, too," they said. "And since his death, we have missed him so much. We'd like to help you and be there for you!"

And now I knew why they'd let Sorn live, and had not killed him right away – it was because he had leprosy, and they were afraid to get near him!

The Cong's were a great comfort to us, and it felt like we had parents again – people willing to take care of us. When I would work in the rice fields I worked closely with them. I was surprised to learn that they belonged to the communist team. How different to see human kindness from communists! They were a close couple, hardly ever apart, and when they were, I could see them looking for each other. They had been through the shock of having their son contract leprosy, and when they told me they were going to help me nurse Sorn back to health, I felt I could believe them.

Days went by, and I was allowed to stay with my husband. I could hardly recognize him at first. He had been a good-looking man, and to see him like this made me very sad. He always dressed so nicely, and now he was very unkempt and from lack of bathing, smelled awful. Eventually other sick people moved into the cabin, and I had to move out.

I was given permission to visit Sorn, but was told, "Only if you fulfill your duties during the day!"

Sorn was a bit better after a month with my care, and the infected sores were slowly healing. He could even be up and walk a little. He mourned for our little daughter, but tried to get stronger and let her go.

After a time, a soldier came to tell him that he must go back to work. "You are assigned to work with the older men, to help build an irrigation system to bring water to the rice fields," he was told.

It was a good assignment, and he was allowed to live in the village again which would mean he'd be closer to me! Yet nothing had changed, people were being killed before our eyes, making us wonder when it would be our turn!

One day when I was working in the rice fields an announcement was made.

In a loud voice a soldier said: "Your new government needs all students, teachers, professors, and previous government workers to step forward. Be honest with us! We want to start the school and hospital up again in the village. The communist government wants to help Cambodia get back on its feet! We can assure you that there will be no more war, guns, or killings. You will be allowed to build homes and be reunited with your families again."

Some of the more educated, and the professionals stepped forward!

And with horror and sadness, we watched as they were massacred! The announcement was a hoax. None of what they said was true! I had been tempted to step forward with them, and let them know what Sorn and I did before communism took over our country. I hesitated and thought, this is too good to be true! And it's a good thing I did!

The soldiers pointed machine guns at them and killed every one of this vulnerable group of people who had fallen for this inhumane trick!

Chapter Eleven

A Soldier Named Ean

We got through each day – meeting whenever we could, though afraid that we'd be discovered, always mourning our sweet daughter, and longing to live together as husband and wife once again. But we were a long way from that kind of normal. I overheard some people in the village saying, "There's something different about Mahm and her husband – they're going to be found out one day and killed!"

Again, we were assembled to witness another massacre! They had tied the hands of their victims behind their backs and blindfolded them! They commanded them to kneel at the edge of a pit – and one by one they were shot, and the bodies of some were kicked into the deep hole. Some were beheaded, their chests slashed open and their hearts pulled from their bodies and thrown away. Some were left at the side of the pit to be dismembered. Younger soldiers would chop off one of the victim's legs, and force them to crawl in front of them. Finding their pitiful movements funny, they'd break out laughing. Tiny infants and toddlers were tortured in front of their parents, who were forced to look on!

Sorn and I stayed away from the soldiers, hiding within groups of people, and pretending to have errands to do in the forest.

The bones and heads were sometimes piled in mounds as a warning to the rest of us still surviving. Starvation was universal, and when that brought on illness, we were given no medicine. Hygiene was a thing of the past! We could not shower or change into non-existent clean clothes, and the only water we had to drink was contaminated!

If we were able to collect rainwater, we had to hide it from the soldiers, and from each other. It was the same with the small animals we managed to catch and kill! We hid the meat from others to keep from starving. Rainwater and edible tree leaves were all we had to survive on much of the time, but we were grateful for these!

When we closed our eyes at night to go to sleep, we hoped we'd survive the night and could open them in the morning. We had forgotten what restful sleep was – so great was the fear that intruded our dreams, we'd suddenly wake up and listen for gunshots and crying, and even when we didn't really hear them, we thought we did!

I trusted a woman who called herself Mae. The soldiers had chosen her husband to be their right-hand-man. I hardly ever saw Sorn, but we had found a secret place in a rice field far away from the village where we could meet. My new friend Mae would sometimes steal rice and meat for us. On such occasions, I would take the food and make my way at night to our secret meeting place, hoping that Sorn would be there. A few times it worked out, and we enjoyed a meal together! But the soldiers found out, and for a while it had to stop! But my wily new friend Mae found us another place to meet!

A month after our latest rendezvous in the forest, I found out that I was pregnant. I should have kept the news to myself, but in my joy, I let Sorn and Mae know! The story leaked out to the communist authorities that we had been meeting and that I was pregnant! We were sternly told not to meet again. Mae told me, "You can't meet anymore! If they see you together, they will march Sorn out of the village and kill him!"

We heard through the grapevine that they were planning to kill Sorn first, and later on me! We dared to meet one last time in a rice field after dark! "You have to leave tonight, Sorn!" I told him, and he agreed.

"I think you should head for Sisophon and from there get as far away as you can! If you can, try to find my parents and give them the news that I'm alive and that Kechara is dead. I wish you could be here with me, but we both know that isn't wise."

We held each other, not knowing if we'd ever see each other again! He walked me to my cabin, and then took off into the night – escaping the certain death that was planned for him!

As I watched him leave I thought, how much more do I have to lose?

I was very close to Mae after Sorn left. She and her husband were the only people that I had in this village to talk to. My fourth month of pregnancy was now starting to show. I looked forward to motherhood again, but wished it could be under better circumstances – I wasn't even sure this second child would get to know his or her father.

It was the job of us women to plant the rice fields. One day as we were returning from a back-breaking day in the fields, a woman whispered to me. She said, "The soldiers are planning another mass killing!"

I started to panic. "Do you know who they are going to kill?" I asked.

"I've heard that you will be among them, because your husband has gone missing," she told me.

There and then, I knew that the soldiers were coming for me that night. Even though pregnant, I couldn't have weighed more than 70 pounds at the time. I almost fainted when I heard what the woman had told me, but quickly I decided: despite my weakened condition, I would escape to save my life and the baby's.

The older couple, Mr. and Mrs. Cong, who had befriended us and helped Sorn back to health had heard that I was to be killed. They came before sunset and told me about a secret route I could take where no soldier could find me. They handed me a "fake letter" to carry, to inform whoever I showed it to that I had permission to visit a relative who was very sick. "When you reach Sisophon, ask for someone named Chark. They help refugees, and he and his wife will take you in and give you help when your baby comes!"

They handed me a small bag of rice, some meat, and a small jug of water. With tears in their eyes, they hugged me and said, "We'll never see you again. Be strong, and you'll be able to save the little life that you're carrying!" And as I walked away, I turned to wave goodbye, and they called, "Don't forget to eat and drink!"

I remembered my last escape, and how hard it was to leave Kechara's grave behind me! How I wished I could tell her she was going to have a sibling, and that soon all four of us would be together again as a family! But that was impossible, only a figment of my imagination.

The recent rains had soaked the rice fields and as I walked through one field after another, my legs would go in up to my knees, making it almost impossible to walk without making a noise! As I pulled my legs out to take my next steps, it would make a 'sucking sound', which I was sure would alert the soldiers to my escape if they were anywhere nearby! I slowed down, and tried my best to wade through the water without pulling my legs clear out.

I prayed to my daughter's spirit once again, that she would be with me and lead me to a safe place.

I started to feel a pressure in my right leg, from the foot I had injured on my last escape. I crawled up on the edge of the rice field to see if my foot was okay; the wound from the nail that had never healed completely had broken open and was bleeding again. I told myself, if my foot gets infected, I might lose my leg!

The pressure turned into pain that shot up to my hip, and I passed out on the edge of the field. When I came to, the pain was so great I couldn't even stand. I had to crawl along the edge of the rice field, rest, and then crawl again. It was easier this way on my foot, but harder on my knees! When I finally forced myself to stand, it felt as though I was carrying a heavy load! My clothes were soaking wet, my baby heavy in my womb, and my wounded spirits just as heavy to carry. The water of the rice fields had sucked many dead bodies into the deep mud, and my whole body smelled of them! It was the rainy season, and a heavy rain poured down, making the border at the edges of the fields very slippery.

I tried to ignore my miserable condition, and let the freshness of the rain invigorate me – when I felt myself falling! In the darkness I couldn't see one step ahead of the other, and when I landed, I found myself in a pit full of bodies!

I finally managed to climb up the slippery sides of the pit! I found a piece of cloth the communists had used and tossed aside to blindfold or to suffocate someone, and wrapped it around my shoeless foot to stop the bleeding.

It was pitch dark as I walked gingerly through the night. And as it does, day dawned and once again I could see where I was going. By this time, I could manage only a few steps at a time, before having to rest my injured foot.

I heard someone whistle. That meant I was nearing a road. I hoped if I could reach the road, someone would give me a ride or at least give me directions to Sisophon! A light rain started, and I got cold! I heard a motorcycle getting closer. I focused on how I would handle the situation if it stopped.

There were three soldiers riding on the motorcycle. And it did stop!

They got off the motorcycle and shouted to one another, "We got her!"

One of them held a gun on me and the other two had ropes and a black plastic bag in their hands. I forgot all about asking for directions! Or getting a ride! Or getting help for my foot!

"Please let me live," I begged. "I am all alone. My first child died recently and I have no idea where my husband is!"

"You can stop worrying about him," one of them said. "He was killed a couple of days ago!"

"Since he's dead and your child is dead, why do you want to live?" another said, laughing.

I knew they were showing off to each other, proud that they had caught me!

My hands were tied behind my back, and I was dragged into a rice field and made to get down on my knees! They started yelling! "You made so much trouble for us! But we've got you now! And we know there are other members in your family that we'll kill after we kill you! Tell us their names!"

I remained silent. They started beating me and threw me down and covered my face with the black plastic bag. I had noticed a mound of dead bodies in the field where they'd taken me, and was sure I'd be joining them soon. The horrible smell made me know they'd been killed only days before. A rope was wrapped around my neck to secure the bag in its place over my head. My arms and legs were tied together. I couldn't fight back, and I couldn't breath! I felt hopeless, and had a terrible pain in my chest! I was crying, knowing that when I died, so would this little one in my womb – I would never know if it was a boy or a girl, and I'd die without saying goodbye to my husband Sorn and my family!

The soldiers shouted their questions! "Where were you escaping from? Where were you going? Is that where your family lives?"

I was so exhausted and frightened, I am not sure what I responded, or if I did at all. I kept hoping they'd shoot me before beheading me or slashing my body as I'd seem them do to my uncle and my cousin. I didn't want to endure torturing.

I heard one of them say, "Hey, let me have her! You've both had your fun, now it's my turn! I'll finish what you've begun!"

I stopped crying, felt a sort of resignation come over me! I am ready to die! I'll soon be with Kechara, I told myself.

Two of the soldiers disappeared, I heard them walking away!

All was quiet! For some time, I didn't know if the other soldier had stayed, or if I was alone. The last I heard them say when they were leaving was, "She's quiet now, maybe she suffocated and is already dead! We'll meet you at the village."

After a while, I felt someone remove the rope from my neck, and take the plastic bag from my head. I lay there in shock, and kept my eyes closed. "Are you okay, Manith," someone asked.

As he untied my legs and arms, I realized he'd used my real name! The one on the LIST!

How does he know my real name, I wondered?

I didn't answer, in case it had been a trick question, trying out a name from the LIST to see if I confessed to being that person!

He felt for a pulse on my shoulder to see if I was still breathing.

I opened my eyes then and looked into his. I recognized him! There was no doubt in my mind who he was! We'd gone to high school together in Sisophon.

"Are you Ean?" I asked.

I'm sure the memory that came to my mind, also came to his. When the high schoolers were on a camping trip, and he was stuck between the rocks in a cave on the mountain we were climbing, I went to his rescue and pulled him out!

"Yes, Manith, I'm the boy you pulled out of the cave," he said.

"When the communists came, I joined their army to save my life, and assumed a new name myself, as I'm sure you have. I have no idea what happened to my family and I've been secretly searching for news about them ever since," he shared with me, showing how much he trusted me. And then, he told me that Sorn was alive, and he told me where he was.

I felt like he had lifted a giant mountain off my chest, I was so relieved! He noticed I was pregnant, and he told me he was going to send me to a place where I'd be safe. Ean gave me food and helped me to rewrap my wounded foot. He gave me some clothes to change into. And then pointed me in the direction of where Sorn was staying.

I looked at him, hesitant to part from such a friend, and said "Thank you!"

He responded with, "You're the first person I've run into from our village, for almost two years. But I keep searching for members of my family that I lost track of during the evacuation!"

"I'll never forget you for as long as I live," I told him.

He handed me another letter to show the next team where I would meet up with Sorn. His last words were, "Go and stay alive! I won't forget you either, because you once saved my life!"

He walked slowly toward the road.

Oh, what a relief! I hadn't been killed – the baby in my womb was still kicking! I couldn't believe that Ean had saved my life! I heard the sound of a motorcycle gearing up, and driving away.

Chapter Twelve

Revealing our Identities

$\mathcal{N}$ow different the rest of my journey was! My foot well-wrapped, felt much better, and I could walk without as much pain. I was dressed in a clean, black dress, with food in my stomach. I had a new lease on life, thankful to Ean for sparing me, and eager to meet up with Sorn!

I continued walking until the sun started to set, and found a secluded spot by the side of the road, and lay down to sleep in peace!

I reunited with Sorn the next day, and we lived in a temporary place with the communist team that Sorn had been working with in the fields. None of the soldiers on this team knew who we really were and I was thrilled to know we were very near my old village of Sisophon. As so often happened because of his skills, Sorn had been chosen to work with the leader in the fields.

I gave the leader the letter that Ean had written, though I had never read it myself. Whatever he told him helped, and I noticed that both Sorn and I were given differential treatment.

Once in a while, Ean would appear, and when he did, he would secretly stop by to see us, and fill us in on any news from Sisophon. We kept our identities secret for almost five months after I arrived to join Sorn. I would soon be giving birth to our second child.

A farmer who lived in the village let me know that my parents were still living in the Sisophon area. I secretly tried to find out more about them from other villagers.

The communist team we had joined seemed completely different from the last four, not nearly as aggressive, but Sorn and I still feared them and didn't let slip in any way that our names were on the LIST.

I was eager to locate my family before the baby came. I wanted them to know about Kechara, and about all the things I'd gone through in the many camps and in my escapes. I wanted to give them the sad news about my uncle, my aunt, and my cousin and how they had died. I wanted to tell them about all the people I'd seen killed, about the pits full of dead bodies, and about those I'd stumbled over in the rice fields. I longed to tell them how much I'd miss my grandmother.

Spring of 1977 was when our second daughter Punleu was born. Sorn was working in the rice fields when she put in her appearance. I didn't know when he would return, but knew that when he saw her, she'd bring joy to his heart as she had to mine! She was so beautiful, and looked just like Kechara. To think I'd given birth to a healthy baby after all I'd suffered during the pregnancy! And she had been born near to the village where I had been born. I didn't have to give birth alone, but was attended by some of the women in the village. After such suffering, this was such unbelievable blessing!

Joy and happiness filled my heart when I held my new baby girl in my arms. I loved staring into her eyes. Punleu brought so much hope and happiness. I grew stronger physically and in spirit after her coming into my life! She made me almost forget that I was still under communism and on a LIST that could change everything in the blink of an eye. For a while I stopped thinking about death and suffering – my fears were temporarily relieved. I forgot about the killing fields, the pits, the cruelties, and just enjoyed my daughter. But I couldn't forget my husband, and was anxious for him to meet his baby girl.

A month later, the men finally returned from the irrigation project they were building, Sorn among them! I was so happy and so ready to show off our second child! The team leader gave Sorn a couple weeks vacation to stay in the village. Our daughter met her father for the first time.

I loved taking care of babies, as I had done in the other villages, while their mothers worked in the rice fields. I was so grateful that I had a good supply of breast milk, and that their babies could nurse and sleep restfully until their mothers came to pick them up. Everything was fine except one thing: my foot wasn't healing, and there was no medicine to treat it.

When I couldn't walk, I scooted! But managed, somehow to help with the cooking and the preparation of food for people in the fields. In this village where people were less persecuted for now, one felt safe and happy, even around the soldiers who we welcomed with warm meals when they returned from the fields. When the women picked up their babies, they'd thank me for feeding them at my breast during the day! I was a good addition to the communist team. They knew their own babies were loved and in good hands with me as their babysitter.

Sorn teased me about having another baby, but I would tell him that wasn't a good idea. "While we're still hiding our identities, we can't be sure about our futures. That's not the best time to have more children," I'd tell him.

It was fun to join other young mothers as we cooked and served in the cafeteria each day. We were happy we could stay close to our babies, and to know that our service pleased the communists. The chief would request I cook things he liked, and I would do it.

All of us were healthy – Sorn, our baby girl, and myself. I was given permission to plant a vegetable garden and to raise chickens. This helped to provide healthy meals to villagers and the communist team alike. They could see I was motivated, and they appreciated my hard work.

However, the infection in my foot made it harder, and harder for me. I needed to find medicine, somehow, to remain on my feet. And when it worsened, I had to stay off it for days at a time.

"I want to build a new cafeteria," the chief told my husband, and Sorn volunteered for the job. That way, he could be close to me and help with our baby. A number of the younger soldiers worked with him and after a couple of weeks the new cafeteria was in operation! It made all of us who were cooks happy – and me, extra happy, that our little family could be together as a normal family for a little while!

We began to suspect the communist chief knew that Sorn and I were on the LIST, but because we were valuable to him, he'd allowed us to continue on in the village, using our fictitious names. And then, one day he asked who we were. Tired of hiding, and trusting the chief, we revealed our identities, hoping it wouldn't bring on persecution or death.

My high school friend, Ean, came back to the village. We were asked to accompany him to the chief's house for dinner. As yet we hadn't heard anything from the chief concerning being on the LIST.

After dinner, Ean came to our house with us and said, "The team leader is not going to persecute you! He told me that the progress in this village – the healthy food and the production in the rice fields is due to you two. For the time being, at least, I think you're safe!"

After hearing that, we tried even harder to stay in the chief's good graces by cooperating and contributing all we could to his team! And then, there was unrest in the village. It appeared the communists were fighting among themselves. The soldiers would shoot some of their own team members!

One day, the chief's wife, who was always friendly with me, came to tell me my parents were alive, and still living in Sisophon. I wondered if they were ever able to leave the village, as my father had planned to do, to escape the communists? *Perhaps one day I'll find out,* I told myself.

Chapter Thirteen

Escaping into Sisophon

The infighting of the communist team provided the distraction Sorn and I needed to slip away. We grabbed up little Punleu, and took off for Sisophon, hoping it was still there.

If it were, we knew it would be under communist control, so we hid out in the rice fields and forests, cautiously making our way. A week later we saw the village still standing! We made our way to the house I had grown up in, and to our surprise it was also still standing, and my family was still living in it. A miracle survival!

A joyful reunion awaited us!

My younger brother saw us first! With eyes as big as saucers, he dropped the wooden toy he was playing with, and started running toward me! He threw his arms around me, and I fell to the ground and started to sob! Hearing his voice saying, "Oh, Manith, are you hurt?" It was like hearing the voice of an angel – unreal and beautiful.

"Wait here, sister, I'll bring Mahrk (Mother) and Papa!" He ran to the backyard, shouting, "Mahrk! Papa! Big sister is here!"

It was late afternoon, and the image coming toward me cast a long shadow, it made my father seem taller than he really was. But I would have known him anywhere. I must have changed, however, for he walked slowly toward me, looking me over carefully, trying to decide if it was really his lost, oldest daughter! I drank in his image, an image I'd seen in my dreams many times, and had longed to see in person! Following him, walking just as cautiously, were my mother, and every one of my siblings – all alive, and looking like themselves!

"I'm Manith!" I said, "It's really me!"

They came running then, and I was surrounded by my longed-for-family, full of happy, big smiles – and tears. We hugged each other like we'd never let each other go!

I was lost in this miraculous reunion, so lost that I completely forgot that Sorn and Punleu were with me!

My favorite brother Sambath was just returning from the river with a bucket of fish, taking in the reunion from a distance. He joined the rest, smiled, and, looking down at Punleu, and asked, "Well, who is this precious little one?"

My precious little one was shy, and clinging to me as if her life depended on it! Sorn remained in the background, smiling at the closeness of our family as it came together after so long a time.

"Everyone! This is 'Punleu' our second daughter! She is almost a year old." My sisters rushed to hold her, and little by little they won her confidence! This was a big moment for Sorn and me. We'd never had the luxury of grandparents and aunts and uncles to love on our babies! My parents waited to have their turn, but eventually everyone had a turn bringing Punleu into the family!

All the kissing and hugging were unfamiliar to Punleu, but I knew in time she'd warm to my eager family. One thing I knew for sure

– no separation, nor hardship, can change the love family members have for each other. We were picking up, it seemed, where we left off!

They wanted to know about Kechara, and what had happened. I told them about the lack of food and medicine, and how her weakened little body had not been able to ward off the malaria that finally took her life. I told them about how hard it was, when I fled the village to save my own life, leaving her alone in the little grave I dug for her with my own hands.

"And how did you end up here?"

"We've had to escape from town to town run by communist soldiers, always careful to hide our identities. Sorn was continually being taken away from me, and I escaped all alone on most of the escapes. In the last village, we revealed our identities and were not sure what would happen to us. Soon after, however, the communist team got into a big fight among themselves, to the point of shooting each other. And that is when we slipped out!

"And you Sorn?" my father asked.

As Sorn shared his own journeys and near escapes from death, his heart-breaking accounts were terribly hard to hear for my parents, and even for me, hearing them once again.

"Why are you limping, Manith?" my mother asked me.

"On my first escape, I stepped on a rusty nail, and my foot has never completely healed," I told her.

"Let's have a look," my father said. He removed the soiled bandage and threw it away. He brought water, and soaked and cleansed the wound, rewrapping it in clean strips of cloth!

After a while he asked me, "Do you feel you could walk with me to visit your grandmother's grave?"

"Yes, please take me to her," I said.

And we took off, talking together as we used to do long before when I was just a little girl and he'd invite me to go with him to see our crops!

I had seen so many elderly people killed and thrown into pits, and mistreated in every way. I was so relieved when he told me that they had shielded Grandmother from the communists, and that she had died from old age, hurried along, of course, by the scarcity of food.

Whenever she was mentioned, it was plain that my family were still mourning her death. I hated to tell them about my uncle, my aunt, and my cousin, but I knew they needed to know, and those deaths added to their sorrow.

I wished I could have been there when my grandmother passed away; she was the person I most admired, and I still lived by the wisdom she planted in my heart. I felt my very survival was owed to her, that any strength I had, and courage, was her careful influence in my formative years! Not only was she my favorite, I knew that I was hers, and held the honor of being her first grandchild – her Kechara. One of the ways I survived the places I had recently lived, was being in the cafeteria, preparing the things that she had taught me to cook! The ingenuity I showed in planting vegetable gardens, and the sewing and mending of the clothing for the communist army, was also due to her tutelage! I'll never forget her having me be co-manager of the family money and the trust she had in me to handle finances. But most of all, she taught me how to love and care for others – even communist friends like Kim, Mae, Reep and the elderly couple that got Sorn back on his feet, the Cong's!

The education I had been hiding in order to survive the communist scrutiny was obtained from all the pep talks Grandmother gave me! The communists had yanked me away from her other admonition, one I had taken very seriously. "Be a role model for your siblings and always take care of them," she's urged!

But now, I thought, by sharing my story with them, perhaps my siblings might be able to survive this communist repression by taking heart in the fact that Big Sister had found a way to survive it!

My grandmother had such a sweet spirit, and a kind and gentle heart. She was known as a provider and a life-saver. She was the best role model one could ever have! The fact that she lived to be 104 during such hard, challenging times, bespeaks a life well-lived!

Just as he had done when I lived at home, before the communists came upon our country like swarms of destroying locusts, my father was always looking ahead. It felt so freeing to be, if only for a short while, under the headship of a kind and loving father, and a faithful, quiet, but constantly-working, mother. And I listened to all that my father wanted to tell me.

"It is very tough, living with the communists," he'd say. "They are not trustworthy, and we have no assurance that our village will continue it's relative safety. As you know, Manith, with each new team, you have to study the situation, and make the necessary adjustments to remain on top of things."

"That's right, Papa. That's how Sorn and I have survived this long – always looking ahead."

"I must warn you, though, my daughter," he told me earnestly, "that this newest team that has come to Sisophon has stepped up the killings. I don't let any of my family leave our home, and I'm continually warning them not to trust, answer questions, or anger the communists."

Punleu was flourishing with all the attention, and was soon taking her first little steps to the applause of her young aunts and uncles! It was as though Kechara had never left me – Punleu reminded me so much of her big sister. Sorn and I made the most of this disarming calmness – which we knew couldn't last. We were happy, proud of our baby, and flourishing ourselves, after having suffered so much since we were first run out of the city!

And then, I had gone to the river for water, and was returning home, when, as I neared the house, I heard yelling and screaming – obviously a big fight was taking place at the chief's house in broad daylight! I could barely make out what they were saying, but heard someone threatening the chief! I heard machine guns next – and the tone of the voices changed, anger replaced with horrifying laments and crying!

I took off running as fast as I could. "Papa," I screamed, "Something is happening at the chief's house."

My father told everyone to hide inside the house and not to come out. Sorn grabbed hold of Punleu and me, and hid with us behind the front door.

The premises of the chief's house were a war zone - bombs exploded, people were running out of their cabins, bleeding and crying, and trying to escape! The bombs had killed many soldiers, and others had been shot. Bullets were flying, and the dead and wounded covered the ground!

"We're too close to what is happening," Papa told us. "We have to leave our home. Quickly, follow me!"

He led us toward the forest. The sky was full of black smoke, and bombs were going off all over the village.

We weren't the only ones seeking refuge and hiding places in the forest, it seemed the rest of the villagers had the same idea! My father, always prepared, knew just where to go. He took us to a place where we were isolated from everyone else.

"Keep very still. Don't make any noise!" He whispered.

I tripped and fell so many times during our escape, that my infected foot started bleeding again! And the excruciating pain returned.

For three days we remained in hiding, everyone helping to keep Punleu from crying. My mother knew that when a baby cries, it is usually from hunger, so she had all my siblings looking for mushrooms – and nibbling on them seemed to satisfy Punleu's hunger, as it did the hunger of the rest of us!

On the fourth night, the infighting between the two communist teams continued!

"We'll have to remain where we are," Father told us, "until everything is quiet again!" So, we settled in on the floor of the forest for another night's sleep, though the gun shots were fewer. "Maybe all will be calm in the morning," he said, trying to instill in us a little bit of hope!

But, the following morning, right before sunrise, they were at it again. Screams and anger spilled over, and their voices carried out into the forest.

"Stay right where you are, keep as still as can be," he said, "I'm going to get a little closer to the village and try to find out what is going on."

When our papa was with us, we all felt calm, but as we saw him leaving, the panic filled out hearts! But we managed to keep quiet, and worked harder than ever to quiet Punleu!

He had walked out, but returned running.

"They're not just killing each other; now, they're killing everyone they come upon in the village."

He took two of my brothers and Sorn with him and said, "We're going to sneak back into our house, and try to bring back food."

Those of us in the forest had our hearts in our throats – wondering if we'd be found out, and fearing the worst! But, an hour or so later, they came back with a big sack of rice, meat and salt. It was plain that we'd have to stay in the forest for the duration of the conflict and killings.

My family were farmers and could survive forever in the forest, if it came to that! Our father had taught all of his children to hunt, both animals and food, when we were young, and we were very familiar with the area. I thought to myself, if we have to hide forever, we're in good hands, my papa will keep us safe, just as he always has!

One morning he went on another reconnaissance trip to the village. When he returned he said, "I didn't see anything but piles and piles of dead bodies! I didn't see a living person anywhere. The piles are made up of a mixture of villagers and soldiers!"

"Do you think it's safe, then, for us to go back?" Sorn asked him.

"Not yet," he responded, "Maybe in a couple of weeks we can move back home

I was so happy to hear my dad say that. Sorn and my father had become friendly, and I realized how alike they were, despite the rocky start Sorn and I had at the beginning of our marriage, when Sorn was so abusive and drinking and gambling heavily. Like my father, though, he'd become very good at figuring out who to trust, and how to maintain his freedom.

The next reconnaissance trip took place about a month after everything started happening. They came back with startling news! "A few families are in the village," Sorn said, "but they're not Cambodian!"

My mother said to me, "It shouldn't be hard to tell where they're from by the language they speak."

A week or so later, Papa led us back to the village. But when we reached our house, there were people living in it! They spoke Vietnamese. And my mother had been right about knowing where people came from by what they spoke!

Always gracious, always understanding, always a peace-maker, my mother spoke to them calmly in Vietnamese. "Welcome to our home," she said. "We have a back room you can live in! We'll all live together!"

Soon our village was an international community with people speaking Vietnamese, Laos and Thai, and we who spoke Cambodian were in the minority.

One day as I was walking alongside the river, I remembered how my cousins and I used to have swimming contests, and how we'd catch fish for my grandmother to fry for dinner. There were miles and miles of this river, but it narrowed to a small creek as it reached our town.

But those weren't the only memories that came to my mind that day, I remembered what happened to one of those cousins! How, when the communists had pulled that black plastic bag off the head of one of their victims, I felt a shock ripple through me when I saw it was the beloved, fun-loving companion-cousin of my girlhood days! I remembered how they slashed him open in the chest and threw him into the river with his arms tied behind his back and draped with heavy chains.

A terrible longing for my cousin came over me. It was he that grandmother trusted to take me to movies. I remember when we were in high school together how we used to help each other with things that were difficult in our homework! We were best friends as well as cousins!

There were no dead bodies floating in this crystal-clear water now! On a sudden impulse, with tears in my eyes, I jumped into the water and started to race with a cousin who was now only a memory! For a minute, I thought I might have gone crazy, until my sister jumped into the river from a rope slung over a tree for that purpose, and we laughed and played and swam for all we were worth – ignoring the fact that the communists would be back!

When we told Mahrk what we'd done, she laughed with us, and said, "I pray every day that Cambodia will one day be back to that kind of normal."

Chapter Fourteen

Sisophon becomes an International Village

People began to once again walk around the village. However, we remained cautious for a long time. Sorn and I, along with my family, stayed pretty much to ourselves, aware of the activity in the village, but waiting to join in.

A new friendliness could be seen in the faces of the men, women and children. And something that none of us had seen or participated in for a very long time was happening: people were joyfully buying and selling! It felt good to contemplate acquiring things again, whether livestock or trinkets, and the motivation needed to work, save and obtain woke up within us. There was a spirit of cheerful co-existence beginning to emerge in the village once again, and a lessening of bad-intentions towards others. Gradually, I began mingling with people, seeking answers to the many questions forming in my mind. Some greeted me and went on their way, but a few, like me, were eager to engage in discussions.

I ran into a few ladies who remembered me from other days and other towns where surviving, or attempting to survive, was our sole occupation. Some wanted to forget it all, but one of them was more willing to talk. I asked her what she knew about the lull in communist activity, and whether she thought it would rise again.

"The tremendous infighting of the communists heightened to the point they couldn't co-exist," she began, "not only between teams, but between members of the same team! What a slaughter! Those who survived evacuated and have, seemingly, just disappeared; but not to stay gone or give up their agendas, I'm afraid. It's more like a time-out to regroup!"

It felt good to find someone who was strong, observant, and objective. She told me that some teams were apparently gone for good, and that people from countries such as Laos and Vietnam were flocking into Cambodia, having heard that the communists were vacating in droves.

"And do you think these foreigners will make this their home?" I asked her.

"No, I think that after realizing how depleted Cambodia is of its potential, and finding all the killing fields with their piles of bones, sculls, and open pits, they'll soon see there's nothing left here for them. That, together with the possibility of a return of the communists, many of them will make their way to Thailand where things remain stable.

"Do *you* think the communist have left forever?"

She smiled at my naïve question, shook her head and said, "The communists are busy gobbling up countries all over Asia, wanting no missing spots on their maps! They'll eventually be back! We all know that there is no safe place here in Cambodia for us!"

But oppressed peoples tend to grasp onto any straw of hope! To hear the general opinion in the village, one would think the evil was done and gone! And now, "Let's just forget it ever happened and get back to normal!"

Of course, that meant a different kind of normal – no hospitals, the medical professionals were all in the death pits. No schools, the teachers were in there with them. No leaders to reform our country – they had been the first victims! No one to really inspire us to reclaim our beautiful culture or the time when we safely trusted one another! Those who could, were now silenced in the killing fields. It was sheer denial to think Cambodia would ever be as it once was!

When those from Laos and Vietnam learned that I could understand their languages, they made friends with me and shared with me why they had fled their countries. They told me it was because communism had used a different approach during the three years of occupation in their lands and had infiltrated the government, rather than destroying it like they had done here. "We've given up all hope of ever having a voice in our own countries again, so we came to Cambodia," they said.

Papa, I thought, could lead a village, maybe even a country, with his foreword thinking – a quality good leadership requires. But he had no aspirations for leadership beyond that of his own household.

What he continually preached from the pulpit of his home when I was a girl, growing up, was the same one he preached now: "Communism is evil. The fact that we are in an apparently safe environment for a time, doesn't mean our village, nor anywhere else in our country, is safe!" And building on that premise, he'd say, "I know that we will all end up getting killed by the communists one day if we stay here! And the fact that we've already lost precious members of our family to communist oppression authenticates my words!" And he'd always end up saying, "We must escape into Thailand!"

Rarely did Mahrk interrupt Papa, but when she did, her words were the exclamation points to his thoughts! "Do you think the Laos and Vietnamese people come to Cambodia to become Cambodians? No, they run the businesses among us, and need us as clientele – taking what little we have left in their own subtle ways. Some got stuck here with the invasion of the communists. Their presence here in our village should not give us a false sense of security. Your papa is right! Listen to him."

"Like us," she continued, "They, too, have lost family members who they loved. And yet to keep us in our villages, for their own gain, the majority of the Laos and Vietnamese among us keep saying that the communists are all gone and will stay gone!"

And then, perceptively, she added, "There are many Cambodian communists currently living right here among us, who through fear, joined the communist army to survive the killing fields. They were never totally committed to a cause, but to escaping with their lives from the atrocities they were forced to commit on *their own people*! They're as happy as we are to be set free, but must be struggling with their consciences."

That made me remember my high school classmate who, as Mahrk had said, joined the communist team to save his own life!

"Mahrk is so right about that," I said, and commenced to tell them about Ean and how he had saved me from the cruelties of his two soldier buddies! And how he had told me he too had assumed a fictitious name, because his real name was on the LIST!

For years our family had been planning an escape from Cambodia, and the time was nearing when we'd have to do just that!

Papa's words were coming true. Once again, the clandestine arm of communism was rising to strike us! More than ever, knowing the LIST still existed, Sorn and I kept our true identities hidden as much as possible in Sisophon. We were careful not to call each other by our real names when around people we didn't know.

And suddenly, the leader of a team showed himself, and announced, "Everyone living in the village must register."

My family ignored the ruling!

Before communism showed its ugly head again, Papa set about improving his farm and orchards! He wanted to give the appearance of staying put! He started working with the palm trees, and orange and mango trees that had survived the burning of fields and properties. All of us helped him to improve our house and fences. We had acquired a few cows, horses, pigs, chickens, and ducks. We adopted two gray watch dogs that we found wandering around, and loved them very much. Anyone watching us would have concluded, that is one family that is staying in the village, there's no need to fear they might escape!

The pain in my legs and feet was gone and I thought, at last the wound has healed! I could play with our animals. Mahrk had given birth to another little boy, and it was fun watching this new baby brother, playing with my little girl who had grown to be a toddler! The balcony of our home was once again full of children, as it used to be!

Papa was determined to continue treating my foot so that the infection would not return. One day he told my mother, "I'm going to the jungle for the herbs I need to take care of Manith's foot!" He had learned from my grandmother just which herbs and roots to use for medicine, and with patience and faith, he seemed to have accomplished what he set out to do!

We knew that war was still in progress in other parts of the country, but life in our village was not experiencing killings at this time. (Perhaps a calm before the storm, we kept thinking!)

It was not as stable as people claimed it was – not like the old days. We felt at peace back then – but now a foreboding of troubles to come lingered with us. I saw everyone trying to make the best of things, ignoring the unwelcome rumors that killings were still happening in other areas. My family's stance was – keep busy, keep watchful, and prepare for escape.

A fifth communist team had arrived who seemed to temporarily allow us to live normal lives. Sorn and I shared our love and labor with my family, and my parents took exceptional care of us. The whole family adored Punleu and of course spoiled her. And I loved playing with my brand-new little brother.

The next thing to remind us that communism was present was when work details began. My father and other men of the village were sent out to relocate dead bodies from the surrounding pits to be put into one giant hole. It took them a month to complete the task, and after that, they covered the giant grave, and filled in the pits. One day I asked Papa, "Why do the communists make you work like a leader in the village?"

"They trust me to do the job and to ask no questions." And then he said, "Whatever I must do to keep my family safe, I will do it!"

Though it was wonderful to be back with a loving father in a relatively safe place, after having felt the evils of communism first-hand, I knew vigilance was still called for.

Be careful, I scolded myself, *don't forget how Kechara died - no food, no medicine, no sanitation; those things could return!* The security I was slipping into was a dangerous place to be. It was important, however difficult, to not let myself forget eating raw meat so that a fire wouldn't give me away were I to cook it, drinking contaminated water because there was no other! We must remain alert!

Chapter Fifteen

Kamol is Born

*L*ife was easier! We'd been living happily with my family for over a year, a much-needed break from constant persecution, hiding, and escaping – and yet, not really a break, because we knew the whole time that someone might let it be known that we were on the LIST!

Having lost one baby, I was very determined that nothing would happen to my second daughter, Punleu! Perhaps I was overprotective, but I had to know where she was at all times, and that this new little love-of-my-life had everything she needed! When I prioritized the things that needed to be done on any given day, her needs were always first on my list! I loved her very much and would do anything to protect her – even die if need be!

For the first few months we were with my folks, Sorn and I were pulled emotionally in different directions! While my family did everything they could to make us happy, we couldn't shake the trauma we'd gone through. Uninvited, a great sadness would suddenly come upon us - our grief was profound for the loss of our daughter. The senseless deaths we'd witnessed, family members who we'd seen brutally killed, the constant fear of being apprehended as someone on the LIST kept pulling us back into the inescapable realities of being under communist control! We knew how hard it was for my family to see us sad, and tried our best to cheer up. When with them, we smiled and laughed, but when alone, we were serious, warning each other not to let our guard down!

Soon, though, it was business as usual in Sisophon! Though work teams existed, it wasn't the hard, constant labor of other teams. People started growing their own crops and livestock again, and buying and selling increased.

As they began to relax, to help them forget the things they had seen and been a part of, many turned to the vices of peacetime – drinking and gambling! Merchants from outside our village saw profit in this and would come in to sell goods, and sit down to gamble with our men!

The hidden treasures of cash, gold, and silver, came out of hiding.

When she was alive, grandmother had her own way of protecting her family's wealth! The men *in her family* couldn't lose it in drinking and gambling, if they wanted to! The money was hidden, and they had to ask Grandmother before any was spent! I knew where her money was hidden at one time, she'd trusted me to help her with it – but I'd been gone for a long time. The good thing about hiding the money was that the communists could not get their hands on it! But now that we were permitted to *use* money again, no one in the family knew there the money was!

My parents would dig around our property, and rejoice when they'd come upon hidden treasures! They'd use it until it was gone, and then excavations began again! Food must be bought, and that depended on money; and, in our case, finding hidden savings!

We went through years of scarcity – never having a full stomach, nor any of the things that made life more comfortable such as oil for our lamps, medicine, blankets, salt – these things were unavailable.

We puzzled over why this fifth communist team had changed so drastically. We were pretty sure it wasn't for humanitarian reasons – and that made us suspicious. It felt good to be buying things that elevated our way of life, but, no doubt, one-of-these-days we were to find out what was up their sleeves!

My papa was proud of how he'd managed to keep his family functioning, even while under the control of the first, second, third and fourth teams. He would move the family between the jungle and the village, depending on the circumstances. He used gold and silver from grandmother's secret burial places to buy food wherever he could, just enough to survive on, if not to fill stomachs.

He managed to keep the family away from where the atrocities were taking place. And he had a way of learning the news and staying ahead of it.

"They're still killing people in the North of Cambodia!" he said one day. "Somehow, it never reached our village, but we knew what was going on in the places where you and Sorn were, and it made us sad."

"But you hadn't heard about Uncle, Auntie, and my Cousin! I hated to be the one to tell you about them," I told him.

Soon after grandmother passed, my family was in hiding in the jungles close to the border of Thailand, and when my dad was telling us about it, he said, "We are jungle people, and it's a good place for us to be when enemies are about! They don't like the jungles!" And then he would smile, knowingly!

Gambling, smoking, and stealing so quickly leads to alcohol abuse! I learned this quickly after I married Sorn. The well-educated, government worker my parents were so proud of quickly fell into the trap of gambling and drinking, and soon began to mistreat his wife and child!

After such a difficult start in our marriage, it took the sufferings we later endured to draw us closer and we never wanted to be apart again. But, to my dismay, in this temporary reprieve from suffering, once again, Sorn was returning to his addictions! Sadly, I no longer mattered to him – nor did his child.

"Manith, isn't it great? I'm winning at gambling, and now I'll be able to help buy food for the whole family!" he'd claim, trying to convince me – but couldn't. A gambler doesn't find it hard to convince himself, however. He always believes the big win is just around the corner! He would invent all manner of lies about why he needed money, and ask to borrow gold from my father. His gambling debts grew and grew, but he just kept gambling!

If he learned that another of grandmother's secret hiding places had been discovered, right away he'd try to get some of it! He became very clever about the lies he told my parents, and at first they would believe him and loan him money. And when his plans didn't work out, he'd be so sad about how someone had tricked him, and they'd feel sorry for him, and go on giving him the money he asked for.

Sorn had spent years suffering from disease and hunger, being separated from me and Kechara, and being put on work teams where they used his talents, only to turn on him again. He'd often have to go into hiding. They were hard years! But strangely, they showed what a wonderful, capable person he really was!

But now, he was the old Sorn, the one I'd fled from when I could no longer stand his beatings.

He continued choosing alcohol and gambling over helping my dad to work around the property, or to repair our home. He even stooped to stealing from my parents, and became an expert at covering up what he'd done with lies! But when my parents discovered that Sorn was stealing from them, being kind people, they would try to reason with him: "Now that you are a father, Sorn, maybe it's time to stop gambling, and get back to work again!"

He would reassure my parents with lies that had to do with me: "When I get enough money, Manith won't want for anything," he'd tell them with his hand out for another loan!

Punleu was close to her second birthday when I discovered I was pregnant with my third child. Had circumstances been better, I would have been happy, but this time I was devastated. And it was hard for me to share this new stress with my parents!

As Sorn grew more and more addicted to drinking, gambling, and lying to us, I began to draw away from him. I grew ever closer to Mahrk and Papa and let them know how much it meant to me to be back in the village with them.

Sorn's and my relationship had not improved, when in 1979, a very healthy baby boy was born in his grandpa and grandma's home. Kamol wrapped himself around their hearts! He was always in the arms of my parents and his adoring aunties and uncles! Before he was born, I kept saying, "I hope it is a boy." I got my wish, and my heart was full of joy! I could tell that my parents were happy about it, too!

Only a month later, we welcomed another baby boy into our home, my sister Manoeum's second child! After seeing so much killing and death, how very blessed we felt to see our family all together and growing! Something we'd never dreamed would take place, especially under communism!

All three of my children were born into this world without their father being present. He could have been there for Kamol's birth, but chose to be away. It made me very sad. I made up my mind to block-out Sorn and his wayward ways, and to retain the joy in my heart of having two healthy, beautiful children, Punleu and Kamol!

(Kechara was very much still alive within me, as well, and always would be the big sister they'd never known.)

My dad became a surrogate father to his grandchildren, since they rarely saw their own dad these days. He was always checking on us to make sure that we were all okay. He would hug and kiss all of his grandchildren. Sometimes, he would put Punleu on his shoulders and run around the house with her to make her laugh. You'd often see him rocking Kamol to sleep in the middle of the day for a nap. My mom loved to feed my children and put them to sleep at night, all cuddled up with her in the hammock. During the day, she'd take them by their hands and walk them around and around the balcony, singing them songs. It seemed to me that this was how it should be! Never having to worry about my children and having my parents with me always. Nothing pleased me more than to see my children in the arms and laps of their grandparents! I lived in a world of love, at last!

Winter was coming, which meant my mother would be busy! As her mother before her, she felt it was up to her to make winter clothes for everyone in her household.

A week after Kamol was born, Sorn came home. He'd been gone over two weeks. He seemed ashamed and at a loss for words – not knowing what to say to me or our children. He came into the house, hungry and exhausted, but he seemed happy to meet our newborn son.

A few days after Sorn's return, we learned that troops of communist soldiers were on their way to the border, to stop people from entering Thailand, and to prevent Thai merchants from coming to Cambodia.

One day the leader of the communist team made a special announcement to the people of Sisophon. "Whoever is found escaping to Thailand will be killed! They will be burned alive or chopped to pieces. Landmines are being planted in the jungles along the border! Be warned!"

The announcement scared those of us who had secretly been planning to leave Cambodia to live in Thailand.

"Here's the interesting thing," my father began, "Your mother and I have been crossing into Thailand for quite some time to buy things for her small business. We use gold and silver to bribe the communist soldiers without any trouble at all."

He let us think about that for awhile and then went on, "So, why wouldn't that work just as well for us to escape?"

My parents weren't the only ones who'd been going back and forth across the border, my father told us, "Merchants from Laos, Vietnam, and other countries have been crossing communist borders all along by paying bribes!"

I thought about what my father told us. I'd seen good days and I'd seen bad, and told myself, *right now they're beginning to tighten the noose! If I want to get away without hanging, now is the time to leave!*

We were always hearing about people who'd left for Thailand and never came back, and I wanted to be one of them. Sorn was so far gone into his vices, and I also wanted to get away from him, with our children. I didn't want to run the risk of getting killed at the border by waiting too long.

My baby son was about three weeks old, and my toddler daughter was growing bigger everyday. I was ready to move! I got up my nerve to share my plans with my parents, "I want to escape to Thailand with the children. And I want to do it alone without Sorn. I can no longer trust him to care of us!" I knew what I lacked was gold and silver for bribing, but didn't want to ask!

I thought much about my marriage. *It's been hard from the very beginning. Off and on we've been together for short periods of time, some of them happy, but something always happens to pull us apart. I know that my parents are willing to support me, but that doesn't seem right. That's not how I want to live for the rest of my life! It's my responsibility to take care of my children, and I want to raise them on my own.*

I broached the subject over and over to my father, and we started talking about finding a way for me to escape to Thailand.

When news reached us that the last communist team was getting closer and closer to our village, and about to move into Sisophon, we became very disturbed and frightened. The feeling of *LET'S GET OUT OF HERE* took over and we felt ourselves panicking. "This is a very dangerous situation," we told each other. All we were waiting for was for my dad to come to a decision about when, how, and where.

Thailand's borders were guarded, we already knew that! Maybe landmines were hidden in the jungles, or it could be just an empty threat! We didn't know for how much longer the soldiers would continue taking bribes – it was anyone's guess! Should I attempt another escape?

Chapter Sixteen

Dangerous Escape to Thailand

*A*fter I shared with my parents that I needed to leave Cambodia for Thailand, they decided it was time for the whole family to take that risk. There was a greater risk now in staying, than in going!

My dad started searching for someone who could lead the thirteen of us across the border. And when he told me his plans, I asked him, "Papa, I want to go as a family, but do you think it is more dangerous for all of us to go at once?"

"Perhaps," he told me, "but let me see what I can find out!"

My father made clear to us that nothing said in our secret meetings about escaping could be shared with anyone outside the family.

"And do not breathe a word of it to Sorn. Who knows, when he is drinking, he could let it slip!" I cautioned.

One day our papa came home and gathered us to tell us what he'd learned. "They tell me that we must divide up in three or four groups. We can't go across the border all 13 at once."

That was bad news, none of us wanted to be separated from each other!

It was finally decided that the first group of three, would be me and my two children. Papa had found someone we could pay to take us right away. We would escape before everyone else in our family!

"There is a refugee camp in Thailand that has been set up by the Thai government named "Khao-I-Dang," my father informed me. "You and the children will be safe there among the other refugees, and you can wait for us to come!"

He went on to say, "I learned that the refugee program is supported by the United States, Australia, Italy, France and Canada. The Thai government will give you the assistance you need, because they have funds supplied by those nations."

"Can you do this?" my parents asked. "If so, you have to go right away tonight with Punleu and Kamol! Can you manage them alone?"

I have to admit, the thought of leaving right away was daunting: I would be all alone, once again! I would be leaving Sorn – wanting to get away from him, but missing the husband who he had shown he could be – both steady and dependable. Would I ever see him again? Would my children ever know their father?

"Yes, Mahrk and Papa! I will go at once. It will be hard with the children to carry, but I can do it if you think this is best!"

My parents started right in, packing the things I would need. A sack filled with gold was tied under my clothing around my waist. A small bag of cooked rice and dried meat, enough for me and Punleu, was put into a bag with the other things I would carry. My sisters handed me a small jug of water! One of my younger brothers handed me another little jug of water and a bag of fruit. Their faces and mine registered sadness, disappointment, and fear.

The man who was to be my guide came after dark. The family saw me off, sad to see me go. I had thought I'd never have to part with them again, but now my I had to be brave for my children, and hold back the tears that threatened to fall! In parting, Dad said, "It's a risk, Manith, but we are all taking risks these days to get away from the evil of communism; there's no other way."

We were very concerned about how Kamol, just 28 days old, would fare on such a long walk. I carried him in a sling close to my breast, so that I could nurse him as we traveled! Punleu was in another sling on my back, which was tightened securely by her Kong (grandfather). I'm sure he wished he was going along to carry her on his shoulders!

"This will be a long, hard journey, Manith, but you're doing what's best for your children. They'll have a broad future ahead of them, rather than the confines and dangers of communism here!" My papa was good at imparting courage! My Mahrk threw her arms about my body with all the slings and supplies, and held us so tightly, as though she'd never let us go! But finally, she said, "It won't be long; we'll see you soon!"

As I walked off into the night, I remembered how my dad promised they would find us in the refugee camp! And how he'd told me, "I've vetted the man who will take you to the border. You and the babies will be safe with him. Just do whatever he says and keep your own opinions to yourself. He knows what he's doing; he's done it many times before."

It had been a sacrifice for my family to let us go first, we had the better chance of making it! Once one member of a family escapes, the rest of the family is watched more closely! I knew also, the first to flee, in all likelihood, would never meet up again with those she left behind. There are just too many variables to escaping that make promises impossible to keep. But they had made the goodbyes easier for all of us!

My guide said little, but when we were away from the house he told me, "No matter what happens, make sure your kids do not make any noise."

He said I must keep them under control, and not let them cry or fuss. It was good that Kamol rode close to my breast where I could keep feeding him. One of Mahrk's parting shots of advice was, "All a new-born wants is milk in its mouth!" I smiled when I remembered that. She'd also made sure that Punleu's pockets were full of bits of fruit and other foods right where she could reach them!

"I will keep them quiet," I told the man!

"Stay focused, don't give way to day-dreaming! Keep your eyes on me – always at attention. Sometimes I may not be able to speak to you, but I will point to things, and show you what you need to be careful of." He went on to warn of things we might come across in the dark.

"Be aware that we will be walking through mud and that the ground is swampy. You might step on a reptile like a snake or frog, or even a fish. Don't let them surprise you, just keep on walking!"

What he said next startled me. "They have planted landmines throughout the jungles. Look for them. That is crucial! And if we happen upon a pit with dead bodies and we step into it, the smell will stay with us a long time. Try not to let it sicken you. Control your mind the whole trip. Think positively, carefully, and be prepared!"

I tried to absorb all his instructions – and not let the many possibilities overwhelm me. I knew that he had to have my complete cooperation and understanding, and that he didn't want me to be weak – and, I told myself, *I won't be!*

It was to be follow-the-leader all the way – and it involved escaping by walking – which had never been easy after stepping on the nail on one of my other escapes! We detoured from main roads, hiking up and down hills, and following winding trails in wooded areas! It only took three hours or so before the pain in my right foot began acting up! I thought for sure the wound had healed, and I shook my head in unbelief! This will make the trip harder and more dangerous, but I will just keep my focus and my eyes on the man in front of me and try to ignore the pain!

After awhile, though, I spoke to him and said, "I'm sorry to have to tell you this, but I'm experiencing pain in my foot."

"We can't rest, and we can't turn back now. We have to keep going," he said. "There's another escape team we're supposed to meet up with at the border that will be joining us and we have to arrive on time!"

I was so confused and bewildered. And complained to myself, *I thought he was paid to take just me and the children? Papa said nothing about another group!* And I asked myself, *what's going to happen next?*

I didn't question him; just kept quiet, and slowed down some as I favored my foot.

And then it started to rain and became very slippery. There was mud stuck to my shoes that I couldn't do anything about, which seemed to aggravate the pain. I kicked off my shoes and started walking bare-footed, which relieved the pain for a while, and I picked up my speed again. The rain finally stopped, but I was cold from the jungle mist and fearful of every step I took, because, with such poor visibility, I couldn't avoid stepping on things that hurt both feet.

I fell into one of the pits with dead bodies. I started to panic because the pit was full of rain water. I had my baby at my breast, and my little girl on my back, and I was terrified that one of them might drop off and drown as I tried to get out. I frantically tried to grab hold of some tree vines and roots to help me, but just kept sliding down deeper and deeper into the slippery mud and the dead bodies. I felt the children's weight getting heavier and heavier. Thankfully, the man leading us had tied me to himself with a rope, and he braced himself and pulled us out!

I was so grateful he'd thought of roping us together, and my appreciation took a leap of growth for the quality of man this guide was.

"Stay calm! Stay calm," he kept whispering. Shivering, cold, and in shock, I was more determined than ever to listen to his every word! And suddenly I remembered what he'd said to my parents when we were leaving: I will do my best to keep them alive and get them across the border into Thailand!

Had he not been so quick-thinking, my children and myself could have perished forever, just a few more dead bodies in that pit!

Before taking off again, he checked the ropes to make sure they were strong, and that we were well-roped together! He looked over the children's slings and fastenings, retightened them and made sure they were covered and secure. He was impersonal, but careful of those entrusted into his care – my children and I were safe and as secure as possible considering all the things that could go wrong.

I knew it was best to travel by night even if it presented more hidden dangers – because the greatest danger of all was to be detected by those we were escaping from.

I tried to ignore what I couldn't help! I had lost my shoes, and I must walk barefoot the whole way despite the pain, and the smell of rotting bodies covering my children, my body, and everything

I owned! I'll keep putting one painful foot after the other, and in time we'll reach the border, I kept encouraging myself!

The two children felt heavier with every mile we took, and sometimes it felt as though I couldn't keep going much longer.

"How much longer to the border," I asked my guide.

He didn't answer me and just kept right on walking. Every step I took was painful, and the exhaustion I felt, deadening!

Like a child eager to arrive where he's going, I kept asking, "Are we going to be there soon?" His whole attention was on avoiding landmines. I knew this, yet kept on, "Will you let me know when we get there?"

"I don't think I can make it all the way to the border without a rest!" I had just finished saying this when I heard one big explosion after another! It was so loud that it woke the baby and he started to cry! I put him on my breast to quiet him. The jungle lit up from the landmines that were exploding.

My guide took off running, pulling us through the darkness. Smoke filled our lungs, as we alternately ran, and hid behind trees. At one point, I caught the shadows of old people, struggling through the jungle; some were lying dead upon the ground with others sitting and crying beside them.

I wasn't sure of just what had happened. I asked myself, are these communist soldiers, or people trying to escape like ourselves? Did some of them step on landmines?

"Don't worry about those people; just keep following me!" I was told in a quiet but firm voice. I tried to walk faster as he ushered me away from the commotion. I felt the ropes pull on my tired body! But before we were clear of the area we would stumble over more people that had been killed from the explosions! My nerves were starting to unravel, as I stumbled along and sometimes fell!

As the sun started to rise, I could sense my guide was more concerned about keeping hidden! He looked toward a field thick with tall grass and took off in that direction. It was harder to walk through, but kept us from being seen.

"Slow but steady," he instructed, "we don't want to make waves to alert the soldiers who are watching the border."

We came to a small pond with clear water! We refilled our bottles, and drank our full! Nearby were trees with edible jungle fruit and we thankfully replenished our bags, and started eating as we continued our journey.

As the sun grew fuller, it grew increasingly more uncomfortable for the children tied to my tired, hot body. They'd been strapped in the same position for so many hours. Punleu fussed to get out of the sling to walk with me. I let her down so she could change her position just for a little while!

"That's not a good idea," the leader told me. "If she runs about the jungle she could step on a landmine! I'm doing all I can to watch for them and she is a distraction. I need to concentrate, try to cooperate with the original plan!"

I didn't need to hear anymore and I grabbed her up into my arms, and, just then, in the distance, I heard a bomb.

"Just a little longer, Punleu, and then you can walk all you want to," I whispered, shuddering in uncertainty!

I gave her some rice and meat to fill her little tummy, and soon she was happy and forgot all about walking.

We were hurrying now to meet up with the other team. If we missed them, we would be stuck in the jungle for a couple more days, the man told me. He knew when the soldiers would rotate their patrol route. It was crucial that we kept up so that when the change took place, we could stop going east, and go in the opposite direction and escape to the west. He had committed to meeting the other team at a certain time. I wasn't really sure how it would all work out, but I supposed I would find out in time. My job was to trust, and follow the leader – that was the original plan!

"Can I get out when we get to Thailand, Mahrk (Mother)?" Punleu asked, softly, and I assured her that she could. And with that, she became more content, and quieted, and was soon fast asleep.

I couldn't believe how little trouble my toddler and my 28-day-old baby gave me, even in broad daylight!

When we finally joined the other escapees, we were lined up single file and told to start walking. The leader of that group was stricter and told us that we were entering the most dangerous part of the whole trip.

"Do not step out of line for any reason. Not even if someone needs help. If you do, a landmine might explode and kill all of us! Besides," he added, "if the communist soldiers find out our secret route they would include this area in their patrol, and we wouldn't be able to lead anyone else across the border!"

I took the words of this second leader very seriously.

A bomb went off not too far from our line of people, as though it was an exclamation point to what he'd just said!

We heard screaming, and people running through the jungle not far away. "Help! Help!" they were calling. We ignored them as we continued single file on our secret route.

We had been told to walk in the steps of the one in front of us. "That way it will appear as though only one person has been walking here," they explained. We were roped to each other so no one would get lost or could pull away from the group. As the leader took a step, I, the next in line, stepped exactly in his track! This technique would convince the communist soldiers that it had been just one of their own patrol.

As we concentrated on how we were walking, we'd continue to hear explosions. We came upon an elderly man and woman. They caught sight of us and came toward us and begged us for food and water. We saw others here and there as we walked. Some looked sickly, others were naked and we couldn't help but feel sorry for them. But we kept walking. We could tell that some were about to keel over and die. I saw a few hanging out of the trees they'd climbed, asking for help getting down. I saw a woman giving birth, all alone on the trail. In one place live babies were crawling on top of their dead mothers, crying to be nursed. But we kept on walking! It was so difficult. We even saw a little boy and a little girl all alone in the woods step on a landmine! The explosion killed them both. I spotted a young teenage girl in the shadows trying to pull off some meat from a dead animal to eat. All along the way these people were begging us not to leave them in the jungle, and to let them come with us to Thailand. But our concentration on how we walked kept us focused; we had to be determined not to give thought to the tragedies being played out all around us!

I was second in line, and felt a deep responsibility to step directly in the footprint of the leader – the rest of the people in the line were depending on me. Though everything within me screamed to help those we passed, I'd promised my guide I would do what he asked, no questions asked – my life, and my children's lives depended on that!

I almost left the line to help the woman giving birth, she was only about five feet from us. The leader sensed my momentary hesitation, and brought me back by saying in a commanding voice: 'No!' Those behind me re-echoed the command, and I closed my heart and stayed my course! "If you pull away, we may ALL die," someone said! And sadly, I realized he spoke the truth!

I so needed to rest, if only for a second, to adjust the slings that held my children. But then the leader whispered, and the message went down the line – "Hurry now, we're almost there!"

I whispered back, "At the border?"

And my heart leapt to hear, "Yes!"

I tried to tell Punleu we're almost there, but when I turned my head toward her, I saw that she was asleep. I was so proud of my children – how tiny they were, but cooperative the whole way.

And then, I could hear sounds from afar – village-type sounds: people talking, cars and motorcycles, cows mooing, dogs barking, and I knew we were getting close to the border of Thailand!

Chapter Seventeen

Khao-I-Dang Refugee Camp

When we heard we were at the border, the whole line of people rejoiced! We envisioned our guides taking us across into Thailand, and all going well! We were anxious to reach the refugee camp where we could relax and feel safe after our long trek through the jungle, dodging landmines, and pits of dead bodies, never knowing for sure if we'd be stopped and killed by the communist soldiers scattered along the border!

The gates we expected to see, which would lead into Thailand were non-existent! Instead, everywhere we looked ahead of us was layer after layer of barbed wire fencing! We knew that by now the border soldiers would have reversed their route, and were on their way back toward our escape route! And we were right! We heard them before we saw them. And when we did see them, they were carrying guns, ready to kill anything and anyone escaping into Thailand!

Suddenly our leader started untying us from one another, and letting us know that we were now completely on our own!

"Scatter about! Keep your eyes wide open! Be vigilant! The only way into Thailand is to run with all your might toward the barbed wire fence. Get through it any way you can, and try not to get hooked by the barbed wire. Pull yourselves free of it if your clothing gets caught, or even your skin! Once you're on the other side, the soldiers can't shoot you, but while you're on this side you are fair game! Be sure of this, left up to the soldiers on this side, you will be killed!"

His final words were, "The soldiers are in the midst of switching their shifts – the only time you have is now, before they finish! GO! Go right now! From this point on, you are on your own!"

My heart almost failed me! Older people started crying, not feeling up to barging through the barbed wire barrier! Confusion and panic reigned! We hadn't counted on our leaders forsaking us!

"I've done all I can do for you! I have to get away from the border before the soldiers come. I can't guarantee your safety beyond this point. Do your best to reach the other side. Good luck!" my leader called before disappearing into the jungle.

Machine guns were set up all along the border, just waiting for soldiers to man them!

From a distance we heard soldiers running, and knew we had been spotted! "Shoot them! Shoot them! Don't let them get across!" I heard them calling to each other!

Adrenalin pumped into my brain, and the fright I felt was of the kind that made me run! I told myself, better to die escaping, than to stand here bewildered and be assassinated! I took off running toward the fence! Suddenly all fear left me, and I really don't know if someone shouted it, or it came from within me, but I heard: Run, Run, don't look back, and don't stop. Don't worry about what you'll do when you reach the barbed wire, you'll know when you get there!

Others were running up and down the border looking for the best place to cross, and I began to hear shots being fired, but I just kept running! I had no idea who lay dying and who continued to run! All I knew was that I was going toward the fence which was looming ahead – ready to catch us in its clutches!

And that unknown voice yelled, "Once you're through the barbed wire, the communists can't overcome you! Go, go, run, run!"

The tall grass in front of the fence helped to hide me from view, and though the soldiers kept firing at me, the smoke created by the machine guns hindered their aim. I felt myself sweating profusely and my heart pounding out of my chest, and I knew I'd never run with such abandonment in my life!

The very last decision I made was, JUMP! When athletes broad jump, they run very fast, so that their jump propels them forward. I'm sure this is what I experienced at the fence, I felt myself sailing over it, and if the barbed wire caught my clothing I have no recollection of it! It seemed I was flying! My children remained roped to my body, but somehow their weight did not hinder the jump I took. I sailed through the air to the accompaniment of landmines exploding behind me, machine guns firing over me, with both soldiers and escapees screaming! I felt a bullet fly past my face – and for a brief moment hoped it hadn't hit one of my little ones!

None of this held me back, not soldiers yelling over and over again, "Die! All of you die!" as they shot to kill those of us fleeing across the border, nor the image of a prickly, dangerous fence ahead!

I don't remember too much after the jump! Everything went dark, whether from smoke or exhaustion, I don't know. I felt blood trickling where the barbs had pulled through my skin, and my legs went numb, and I couldn't feel them. I felt my little daughter still on my back as I fell, and knew I had landed on something hard! I landed face down on the ground, and I felt a tiny little leg moving underneath me, as if it was struggling to be free. I realized that I had landed on top of my baby boy, but I couldn't do anything about it. I just lay their helpless with my eyes closed.

My mind focused on Kechara, my uncle, my aunt, and my cousin, and I told them, this escape is dedicated to all of you!

My crossing into Thailand is to honor them, and all the other Cambodians who have been massacred and murdered by the communists. I have jumped for all of them!

And then I passed out, and no doubt Punleu and Kamol had also. How long we lay there, I'm not sure. Finally, I heard a woman's voice, saying: "Ma'am, you are on top of your baby, can we help you to get up?"

I came to, and slowly I turned my head and looked up. I saw only the shadow of a person. My vision was not clear and I didn't know what to do – how to respond.

"Where am I?" I finally asked.

"You are in the country of Thailand. You're safe now, and you are with a Red Cross team," she said. "Please let me help you and your children," she kept insisting.

"Will you let us untie your children, and get them cleaned up?"

Punleu was trying to get free of my body, for she, too, was face down, and was wanting to turn right-side-up! Several others came to help the first lady, and I could tell I must be in Thailand because they were speaking Thai! They kept telling me, "You're safe now!"

I was still helpless, but I thought, at least I understand Thai, I know what these people are saying!

As I became more aware of things, I realized I was laying on top of Kamol, but was going to need help getting my own self right-side-up in order to rescue him from my weight.

I didn't immediately trust the Red Cross team, but soon they took over and righted our situation. The man on the team tried to sit me up, one of the ladies picked up Kamol, and the other held Punleu in her arms.

I was drained of all the adrenaline that had propelled me across the border, and now I was very weak; I couldn't walk. The man picked me up in his arms and carried me to a trailer, he freed me of all my bundles. I kept reaching out toward my children. I was so afraid we'd get separated from each other, and I'd never find them again.

"They are in very good hands," a Thai lady told me, "as soon as they're cleaned up we'll return them to you."

I was still very confused, and kept asking them if we were in Thailand, and they very patiently kept telling me that we were. When the numbness left my legs, and I could walk again, I saw that the trailers all had banners on them saying: Red Cross! I was being walked from one place to another.

All of the people inside the trailers were dressed in white gowns, and I started to recognize that most of them spoke Thai! And I began to relax and felt a gentle happiness overtake me.

I was given soap and directed to the showers! The water mixed with tears of relief washed over me and I felt so clean and so refreshed. I had not had a shower in many, many, many months! I was given several sets of clothing for myself and for my children!

After we were clean we were taken to another trailer where we were given shots, and other needed medications. When I was reunited with my children, I was amazed at how beautiful they looked. They smiled when they saw me, and Punleu showed me the food in her hands! For a whole day we were left in a trailer to rest.

It's hard to explain how I felt. For the first time in many years, I was free from the threat and oppression of communism! The Red Cross is a real organization, doing what they profess to do, and their help was something I had never in my wildest dreams expected to have! Not only were they helping me medically, they were guiding me and helping me to feel that I was, in their estimation, a worthy person!

"The next step," one of them let me know, "is to register for the Khao-I-Dang refugee camp. They need to know the name of the country you have escaped from."

We entered the refugee camp, and were taken to a good-sized, one-room hut, which had bamboo walls and a thatched roof, woven from palm leaves. This clean, comfortable dwelling was provided by the Thai government, we were told. It was supplied with canned foods, fresh fruits, supplements, fresh milk, and medicines.

After we settled, the following week, I met people from other countries, like Laos and Vietnam. We were all welcomed and treated the same.

After about a month in the camp, I spoke to some of the Red Cross workers I had become acquainted with, and offered to work with them. They accepted my offer, and I worked as part of the Red Cross team, cleaning and helping to prepare food. As the weeks passed, my children and I started to feel much better. When I worked at the clinic, the doctors allowed me to bring my children to work.

I looked forward to my work with the Red Cross. I helped to welcome refugees from other countries. The majority of the Red Cross team spoke English, and I began to pick up more of that language, and what I'd learned in high school began to come back to me. It was a wonderful experience working every day, and most of all, to feel so safe!

But sometimes late at night, after the children were tucked in, I would remember my escape and running toward the border of Thailand. I would go over it in my mind and ask myself, how did you run so fast bearing the weight of your two children? How did you have the courage to dodge the bullets of the machine guns? I would replay in my mind the hateful words of the soldiers: 'Die! Die! Die, all of you!'

And as I replayed the escape in my mind, I could almost smell the smoke, and feel myself flying through the barbed wire with utter disregard for what would happen to us – and landing with a thud! And then, I remembered the calm and kindness, the shower, and the fresh clean clothes! The tender exam of the doctors! The assurances that we were going to be okay.

I tried so hard to remember every detail. The Red Cross doctors knew that the horrible memories of the escape would come back again and again to haunt us, and part of the way they helped us in the Refugee Camp was learning to deal with our trauma. It was a process, they explained, facing what we'd suffered and then really believing that we were going to survive! PTSD (Post Traumatic Stress Disorder) affected us all and was treated in the refugee camp.

When I asked one of the doctors if I could go back and see the border one more time, his answer was, "Yes, of course. Seeing it again, will be alright, but let's see if you can begin to replace those moments with new, healthier memories!"

155

On that last visit to the border, there were Red Cross personnel with me when I broke down and cried, not only from sorrow but from anger! I saw communist patrols marching along on the Cambodian side.

As I looked into the eyes of the soldiers, I saw the eyes of devils, they were not humans, and they had no mercy and seemed to delight in killing as many people as they could. Here and there were mounds made up of the bodies of those that had been killed trying to cross the border, and of those who had been victims of landmine explosions.

I looked at the rows of barbed wire fencing, only this time, from the safe side, they didn't look as menacing – I could almost see my body, thick with bundles, lying on the ground, and the three people who had come to rescue me from the cords that bound my little ones to me. I felt again the numbness, the half-conscious stupor as each of the three merciful Red Cross people carried a member of my little family to the medical trailer where we had our first examination.

I replayed in my mind being examined and treated by the medical team as they discovered embedded in my head and arms, shrapnel from the landmines and bullets that exploded during our escape. The chaffing and rubbing of the sweet bundle on my back had made sores and cuts, and the barbed wire had done its part also; the black and blue bruises would take a while to fade!

I looked at the barbed wire fence again, and tried to imagine the members of my family trying to surmount and get through it, and I couldn't believe it would be possible, and I fell to my knees and screamed in anguish. My heart was in so much pain. I was so sad and I felt such a great loss in my heart.

The Red Cross personnel that had accompanied me tried to comfort me.

"Manith, you saved the lives of your two beautiful children! You mustn't give up on your family – they will find a way, just as you did!" said one.

"Give it time! Have patience!" said another.

They returned me to the camp, and I never asked to go back again! And I found a way to do what they asked and continually told myself, if they decide not to come, may my parents continue to protect and guide my siblings where they are! And if they do come and make it to the border, may they have a good guide, that by then will have found a better way to cross.

The benefits of the Refugee Camp were many. No one was forgotten, not even the children. Punleu had never had such toys before as the ones she was given by the Red Cross. We were allowed to stay as long as we needed to, which in my case, I planned to do until my family arrived! I didn't have to worry about food, medicine or a place to live! When they knew I was interested in learning English, they provided me with lessons, and materials!

The Thai government opened their doors to us, allowing for us to stay in their temporary housing. They built three refugee camps, and began retraining refugees, on how to live again as free people. I registered the first time soon after entering the country, and was required to register for the second time as a refugee from Cambodia.

I understood Thai, Vietnamese and Laos and had studied English and French in school. I found myself using all of those languages as well as Cambodian as I interpreted and translated for the medical staff and the refugees being treated. My English was used constantly in the clinic, and I became more and more proficient all the time in that language.

I considered becoming employed as a translator for the Thai government or the Red Cross if I decided to stay in Thailand.

Though my basic health kept improving, my foot remained a major medical problem. From the constant infection over the years, the skin began falling away, until I could almost see the bone. I showed it to the Red Cross doctor. He told me he needed to keep an eye on it, and put me on medication that I would take every day.

Punleu and Kamol were getting healthier and were favorites with the Red Cross staff. I started talking to my children in English, and before long, they began understanding and speaking it, as well — which delighted the English-speaking Red Cross workers.

I watched all the incoming refugees, hoping that one day, I'd see someone from my family! Three months passed, and still no one! I knew they would come through Khao-I-Dang, for that is where all the Cambodian refugees entering from the south were assigned. There were two other refugee camps, but the Thai government and the Red Cross did not station any new arrivals there. No, if they got across the border, I would definitely be reunited with them.

Khao-I-Dang, was the camp for new arrivals and the people living there must stay for at least two or three years. The Thailand government and the Red Cross made sure that the refugees kept healthy, learned new languages, and were able to work when registered as refugees. Only then could they transfer to other camps. Each refugee was carefully processed, and records kept on each one's progress.

The Red Cross team was always giving 'pep talks' to motivate the refugees. Their interest in me was a great comfort. It was almost like being a part of a family!

One of the pep-talks went something like this: Don't worry so much about your family in Cambodia. Let it go for a while. Let it go completely, even though you are alone with your children. Keep your mind on things that are actually happening, the progress you are making, and the goals you are setting for your own little family! Concentrate on the refugee camp, and helping others to adjust!

Sometimes Red Cross personnel would ask me if they could take my children with them to market. And while they were out, they'd spoil them with food, toys, and clothes. And though I never left the camp myself, Kamol and Punleu knew all about the outside!

I grew especially close to one of the American nurses named Alice. She liked me and offered to teach me English. She loved to spend time with me. I began going early each morning to the Red Cross trailer to practice speaking English with her. When she saw the children were a distraction, she arranged for someone to watch them so I could focus on English.

English had been hard for me when I was in high school; it was required in high school if you wanted to enroll in college. But now, studying with Alice, it was not hard at all! When she saw I could manage studying two languages, Alice introduced me to French, also. She knew that if I grew really proficient in these languages, it would help the medical team greatly to communicate with new arrivals. She said she felt lucky to have me, and I told her that I felt lucky to have her! She was a wonderful teacher and a very good friend.

As our friendship grew, I began to open up to her, and share things about my life.

"Are you married?" Alice wanted to know. And I told her I was, but that my husband Sorn's addictions had led me to leave him and to escape alone with the children.

"But," I told her, "another reason I had to leave Cambodia was because I was on the LIST of those that the communists wanted to kill." I explained to her that anyone with any type of education,

159

whether professionals or government workers, were all on the LIST. "My husband is on the LIST, also!" I told her.

"He put us both in danger because of his drinking. I never knew who he might be gambling with, and in what unguarded moment he might divulge that we were on the LIST."

I told her about the deaths of my uncle – a medical doctor, my aunt – a nurse, and my cousin – a police officer.

"When Sorn began to steal from my parents, and engage in other erratic behavior, like disappearing for weeks at a time, it put my life in danger," I told her, "and that is when my parents wanted me out of the country before it was too late, and it was discovered that I was on the LIST of people to be killed."

I told Alice that I wanted to start a new life and to give my children a more secure future, where their father could not find us.

Though she was still single, without children, I could tell that Alice felt compassion for me in my difficult situation. She was a constant comfort, support and encouragement. Whether our paths ever crossed again or not, I would always count her as one of my best friends.

I worked with the Red Cross under Alice's supervision for about six months, translating what Cambodian refugees had to say about their health conditions into English or French, so that she could treat them. Because they saw me when they came for medical help, I gained the respect of my fellow-refugees, and many friendships developed; we all learned to help each other.

My foot was getting better and healing enough so that I could walk without pain. Eventually, I was permitted outside the camp when Alice would invite me to come along to purchase medical supplies in the small Thai village nearby. I was paid in canned goods and fresh foods each week. In the refugee camp, we didn't use money.

I sometimes exchanged my canned food for meat with Laos or Vietnamese refugees.

A year went by, without a trace of my parents and my siblings! For the most part, I resigned myself to wait for the right timing, and my life was full and happy. I would ask Alice for any news on new arrivals from the border, but the answer was always - no news.

Now that my life wasn't in danger, my family characteristics began to blossom again. What I learned from my role models – Grandmother, Mahrk, and Papa – took over my personality. I loved serving people by sewing, cooking, and encouraging them.

But the thing I enjoyed most of all, what was my passion, was teaching refugees how to read, write, and speak in English and French. I started to teach a beginner's class of English and French. Before long I added some conversational classes, and soon many were able to carry on simple conversations with the Red Cross personnel. I also taught some how to make their own clothing, and how to prepare certain kinds of food.

And then I thought maybe we should formalize the teaching; in order to do that, we'd need somewhere to teach. I began a search for other volunteers who could teach the skills they had learned. When I shared my idea with the Red Cross they honored it, and told me, "We will request a 'building facility form' and forward it to the Thai government for approval."

The Thai government gave its approval within a month, and the building of a school facility began in the refugee camp. I was so happy. When it was finished we used one side for children, and the other for adults. We acquired six volunteer teachers for the learning center. I loved to see my daughter get ready for school every morning. She enjoyed learning and sometimes wanted to boss the whole class to everyone's fun and delight. I loved the volunteers who were willing to step up and teach alongside me.

I could hear grandmother's lecture: getting an education is very important, Manith!

Wouldn't grandmother have been proud of my part in making education available at a refugee camp, I told myself!

And the more I taught, the more I learned personally.

The facility soon filled with people wanting to learn. When the classrooms were outfitted with tables, chairs and a black board, it took on the appearance of a real classroom! The facility held about forty people.

When I reflect on this time, I give a special thanks to the Thai government, for providing all the school supplies, and giving us forms to request whatever we needed to replenish them. With no formal training, the other volunteers and myself devised our own lesson plans from our own days as students, incorporating the things we could still remember.

Each day, except Fridays, reading, writing and language classes were taught – French and English were in demand. Friday was for creating! We cut and sewed, making our own clothes on some Fridays, and cooking on others. Not too many men came, but most of the women loved Fridays for all the fun and fellowship!

The Red Cross personnel loved when we cooked Cambodian dishes. They would come to the school to taste our food! They even liked to have us make clothes for them. Close relationships were developing between the refugees and the Red Cross workers.

I wasn't the only volunteer in our family. Punleu loved to imitate me. She'd pick up a little stick, strut around the classroom and act the part of a great teacher. "Listen," she'd command, shaking her little stick at the older students, who would laugh at her cute little antics. The friends she met in the classroom, she played with out of school on the weekends!

Punleu was only two years old. She loved her little brother and wouldn't share him with anybody. It was wonderful to have no conflict in our little home in the refugee camp – we were truly happy. It was a regular utopia – all our needs being met by the Thai government and the Red Cross.

Because of my language classes, the quick learners were soon conversing in English or French on their own – not needing me to interpret for them!

I gave the names of my parents and siblings to the Red Cross team who received and registered new arrivals to Khao-I-Dang and would ask them from time to time if any of them had entered, but the answer was always, "Not yet!"

Chapter Eighteen

Under a Shady Tree

Some of the refugees in Khao-I-Dang were moving to a transit camp called Kam-Put. It was the camp where refugee families waited to be transported as immigrants to countries whose doors were opened to them. Some of the refugees hoped one day to be citizens of Thailand and they remained in this first camp, but those who had submitted applications and requests for sponsorship to other countries moved to Kam-Put.

One day, on my way to the learning center, I saw a group of people gathered under a tree. I stopped and went over see what was going on. One of the men was very tall, and he held a thick, black book in his hands. I was surprised to hear him speaking English. I observed what was going on, and tried to understand what he was saying. He read some from the book, and then seemed to be explaining it to the others who were gathered. I was pretty sure that not all of the refugees could understand him.

I spoke quietly to one of the women, and asked, "What is he talking about?"

"He's talking about Jesus," she answered.

"Who is Jesus?" I asked her. "Does he live in this camp?"

"No," she answered, "Jesus is who he is reading about in his book."

"Where did the book come from?" I asked. "I'd like to read it."

"You'll have to ask the man," she said, "He comes every Sunday morning and reads the book to us and then he tells a story about Jesus."

When Sunday came around again, I went and sat under the tree, waiting for the people to show up. When the tall man arrived, he walked straight over to me. I stood up and said in English, "Hello."

He looked surprised, and he asked, "Do you know how to speak English?"

"Yes," I responded, "I speak a little English."

"Welcome, Manith," he said, extending his hand to shake mine. "My name is Paul Williams."

"How do you know my name," I asked.

"Oh," he said, smiling, "the Red Cross workers have told me a lot about you."

"Tell me about the book you bring with you," I said.

"This book is called the Bible," he answered, holding it up, "And there are many stories in it about Jesus. I hope you'll join the others who come each Sunday, and listen to some of the stories about him."

"I will stay and listen to your story today," I said.

By then, other refugees started coming to the tree, and I sat down among them, and was soon listening to the tall man read from his book, and to his story about Jesus. He handed out pamphlets after the story, and I took each one he offered, and returned home with a handful of free reading material. He told me to read them in my spare time, explaining, "They are all about Jesus, and from them, you can know more about him, too. Do come back next Sunday."

I don't think Paul would have approved of how the pamphlets were used once they reached my cabin – not for learning, but for fanning my children to sleep on hot nights.

The next Saturday, I decided not to go anywhere, but instead, to tidy things up in our shelter. I got busy, putting things in place, cleaning, washing, and dusting. When I finished, and was arranging the pamphlets on a shelf, I became curious, and picked up one of the pamphlets Paul had handed me and started to read it, in English, of course.

The one I chose was the story about the birth of Jesus. It said he was born from a virgin woman that had never had a husband, and that he came to save the world. At first, it was just a story, and it didn't concern me very much, but then, I asked myself, did this child really exist, or is he just a character in a story? And what was he saving the world from? Maybe communism? Maybe I should ask the tall man named Paul about this.

I met Paul's wife who came with him the next Sunday. Her name was Wendy, and she was as friendly as her husband. I asked them my questions, and they told me to stay after the meeting, and they'd tell me more about who Jesus was and why he came into the world.

Paul offered to bring me a Cambodian Bible the next Sunday. "I think it will make more sense to you to read about Jesus in your own language," he told me.

The next Sunday he presented me with my own Bible, in my own language! There were eight other people gathered with me, along with Paul and Wendy. Whenever he'd read in English, I would follow along in Cambodian. We all sat under the shady tree and studied the Bible together.

"Would I be able to meet Jesus in person?" I asked Wendy. "Could you help me find him?"

Paul and Wendy did not respond; they just smiled at each other.

When I was studying English with Alice, she had given me an English Bible to use to practice reading in English. I started studying the Bible on my own by comparing what it said in Cambodian with what was written in English.

Paul and Wendy wanted to learn to speak Cambodian, and I was still working on English. So, we started helping each other! They'd listen to me read from my English Bible, and correct me, and I'd listen to them read from their Cambodian Bible, and help them to pronounce the words correctly. All the while, my Red Cross friend Alice continued my lessons in English. Just as I'd done with Alice, I became more and more comfortable around Paul and Wendy, and they with me. We were all very happy when we saw each other progressing in the languages we'd set out to learn!

When a Thai missionary saw what was happening, she asked if I would help her to learn to speak Cambodian, as well. And I had another pupil.

Paul and Wendy Williams were from the United States. They were with the Southern Baptist Mission, and had been working in the refugee camps for many years to spread the gospel of Jesus Christ.

My life was very full now, and happy! I taught every day at the learning center, concentrating on teaching languages, sewing, and cooking. I had others volunteering to help me with both adult and children's classes. It was a heavy schedule for me, for sure, but it was so fulfilling to see people who had once been suffering under communism, now free to learn once again, and to share their learning with others.

One day I had a discussion with Paul about the people transferring to the Transit Camp. (He referred to it as 'an opportunity camp.')

"Well, you are certainly taking advantage of opportunities in this camp," he smiled. "You're working with Alice in the Red Cross office. You're teaching at the learning center. And Wendy and I are very proud of you, and all the ways you help us."

That made me happy to hear. And what he said next made me smile.

"Wendy and I love to be with your children, too! You can tell that you don't neglect them to do all of the other things you do. They're so well adjusted!"

A few families who had been students at the learning center said goodbye to me one day, telling me about their transfer to the Transit Camp.

I was sad and yet I knew I'd have to let them go, with my blessing. They must move on in order to reach their goals! One of the reorientation precepts we'd learned in Khao-I-Dang was to set goals again! Our only goal for so many years in our own countries, which had been taken over by communism, was to survive and escape! And now, free from persecution and fear, we could once again plan futures!

One of the things I'd heard about the Transit Camp was: 'They give you beds and you don't have to sleep on the ground!' And I thought, that is going to be one of my goals now! Even a hammock would be better than the ground.

A Red Cross worker came to the learning center one day and said she needed to speak to me. She took me aside, and said, "Manith, there's a new arrival, claiming to be your husband."

I excused myself from my class, and went with her to see who it was, and if it truly was my husband. I was excited, because I thought, if Sorn is here, maybe my parents and siblings are here, too!

We reached the Red Cross trailer and I looked inside, but saw only one person! My husband Sorn! At first I didn't recognize him. He looked so different. He was very thin and unkempt.

"Yes," I told the Red Cross worker. "That is my husband, but he looks sick!"

We took him to my cabin. After he was cleaned up, we fed him.

I can't say I was happy to see Sorn again; in fact, I'd hoped never to see him again! I'd been looking forward to reuniting with my parents and siblings – but when my escape was planned, it was to be alone, so that I could raise my children without their father's drinking, gambling, and abuse. I didn't know what to say to him, and he seemed to be uncomfortable with me as well!

"Did you escape alone?" I asked. "Did my parents come with you?"

He said, "I came alone." And then, he went on to tell me, "I returned to Sisophon after a time, and went to your parent's house – but it was vacated, and when I asked some of the villagers where they were, I was told they had escaped to Thailand."

I didn't dare think about what had happened to my parents and siblings! Since they had not arrived in Khao-I-Dang Camp, they might have been killed at the border! For my father had assured me that if I reached the refugee camp, that is where we would find each other! I was devastated.

I looked at Sorn, and asked myself, *do you want to risk letting a husband back into your life that brings with him the addictions and troubles that caused you so much suffering?* I knew that I had to decide, and ended up feeling sorry for him, and asked the Red Cross worker to help him.

It was discovered that Sorn had tuberculosis. I was very concerned for myself and our children, that perhaps we would catch it from him, and asked Alice about it.

"We'll get him on the newest type of T.B. medications right away, which will hurry up his cure, and protect your family from contagion," she assured me. And so, our little family was to be reunited!

I probably would never know all the details of how Sorn made his escape alone. It wasn't long, though, before I could see bonding taking place between him and his children – they were very happy to meet their father, and he to see them once again!

The next Sunday morning, I told Paul and Wendy that my husband had arrived in camp. Without going into any detail about my own misgivings, they assumed I was happy about being reunited with Sorn.

"We're so happy for you, Manith, and for your little ones!" they said.

One day Paul and Wendy said some things that started me thinking!

Wendy said, "We've just heard that President Ronald Reagan has announced that the U.S. government is accepting refugees from Thailand and other places."

Paul asked, "Have you ever thought of going to America to live, Manith? I'm thinking your family could have a blessed life there. From what you've told me about your husband, he shouldn't have trouble finding work, and you, for sure, could get work with all the skills you have."

I was excited and wanted to hear more about how we could make that happen. Every time we'd get together, I'd pepper them with questions – about the country, the people, the customs and culture! "Can you show me where America is on the map?" I asked them.

And when I saw where it was in comparison to Thailand I realized it was far, far away, and that if we were to go, it would be forever! Sobering thought!

"The country is well-run, and the people are, for the most part, hard-working," they told me. "In fact, usually both husband and wife bring in income, especially when they are first starting out. There are many schools, universities, and on-job-training opportunities, to better yourself."

And using one of his favorite expressions, Paul said, "It's a land of opportunities!"

Paul and Wendy knew that it had to be a family decision, and that one member couldn't make the decision alone. "Talk it over with Sorn, and find out what his thoughts are," they counseled me.

Sorn and I talked it over. We could make a whole new life for ourselves, and since we'd given up hope of ever seeing a change in government in Cambodia, it seemed the best thing we could do – however, leaving Thailand, would be cutting all ties with our own country forever.

"Let's do it," I said, and Sorn agreed.

I went to Paul and asked him to help me fill out the applications and to submit them to the United State's government.

After setting things in progress, though, I began to reconsider. It's going to be hard to say goodbye to all the Red Cross workers, and especially to Alice! I'll have to leave the learning center and all the people my life has touched there.

On the one hand I was ready to move forward, but on the other, I was hesitant to leave the known for the unknown. There was a mixture of excitement and sadness. Those I was reluctant to leave were the very ones who were encouraging me to move forward – telling me I had their support! That, when they could, they'd visit me, and they assured me that I'd make new friends wherever I went.

Paul and Wendy promised me that they would be on hand in the Transit Camp to help me adjust, and be there for my children. They would see that we received the proper care, and that all our needs would be met.

Chapter Nineteen

Our Life was Changing

A couple of months after submitting our application to the U.S government we moved into the Transit Camp. The Red Cross, having treated Sorn for tuberculosis, could verify that he was exempt from a disqualifying disease, a requisite for residence in Kam-Put.

The countries that had offered asylum to the refugees that had escaped from communism into Thailand were the United States, France, Canada, Australia, and Italy. The Thai government had built the Transit Camp for those who awaited acceptance from one of those five nations. We were all very thankful that, since we could not return to our own countries; there were other places we could go to where we could put down roots again without fear.

Paul and Wendy kept their word, and were such a blessing to me in the Kam-Put Camp as I prepared my family for relocating in the United States.

The time I spent teaching Cambodian to Paul and Wendy was not in vain! Every time they came to visit us they'd greet us warmly, with big, friendly smiles, in our native tongue. I could always expect hugs from them, and gifts – many times fresh fruits and other foods from the outside markets. I noticed they had also picked up a lot of Thai as well.

It touched the hearts of the Cambodian and Thai people that these Americans were learning our languages. I knew that once we reached the countries we were going to, we'd have to learn those languages, and I hoped I'd be as eager to do so as Paul and Wendy had been to learn mine!

I loved going to the Bible studies hosted by Paul and Wendy. I had never thought of God and his attributes before, and they made it plain to us that God was greater that any of us, even greater than Buddha and the other gods our people worshiped. But the thing that amazed me most was that this great God *loved us* so much. He even sent his Son to earth to tell us about Him. I had no idea that God cared that we sinned, and that if we sinned we couldn't go to his town in heaven. And it touched my heart that his Son knew this, and wanted to take our punishment. Not only did this God love people, he forgave their sins when they believed that his Son died for them.

Paul made things as clear as he could – using English, French, Cambodian and Thai – so that we could understand. He welcomed our questions, and always answered them with Bible verses. I still remember when I realized what sin was, and how I could ask God to forgive me of mine.

That God loved me, was the message I came to believe, and I think I believed that because of the wonderful Southern Baptist missionary couple into whose arms I had fallen, seeking love, comfort, and guidance!

I continued reading in both Bibles – Cambodian and English! It helped me to understand better having both versions. I hadn't ever before felt such peace in my heart. I knew that it was God who was bringing it to me, because I was believing his Word, and trusting in Him.

I had not lost my Red Cross friends, like Alice, and I still appreciated them very much. But it was different with Paul and Wendy. I didn't know the scriptures yet about Christians being a family, but when I look back I realize that this couple who watched over me were my new siblings; I felt they would do anything to support me and my children! They truly would go above and beyond to show me God's love. They were real, and true friends.

Every time I couldn't understand something in my Bible reading, I'd go to them with my questions. I didn't realize it, but my faith was growing. I wanted to see Jesus. I wanted to speak to him in person and say thank you to him for dying on the cross for my sin. And that is when they let me know about prayer.

Paul and Wendy never preached to me, or pressured me, but they guided me, and would show me the verses in the Bible that could answer my questions. I began to pray – a brand new experience for me. The prayers we said to Buddha were learned prayers, but this was a God I could talk to like a father! I started praying that God would give me understanding, and to keep hope alive in my heart. I continued working on believing what I read to be true, and my faith in God kept growing.

Kam-Put camp was about twice the size of Khao-I-Dang. There were many more refugees there. It was a much cleaner environment, and, just like I was told in the first camp – here we didn't sleep on the ground.

In Kam-Put we didn't have individual cabins as we had in Khao-I-Dang. The Thai government had built a number of large buildings, called homes, for us to live in. Each building was built above ground, with compartments for individual families.

Shortly after Sorn and I, and our two children moved into the Kam-Put Transit Camp the Red Cross workers arranged for us to meet some of the other new people in the camp. I was so impressed, everything was so clean. I saw several other tall facilities with signs above them. One read: Learning Center; another: Red Cross; and yet another: Southern Baptist Mission, United States of America.

I ran to the last building, went inside, found a door with: Paul and Wendy Williams written on it. I knew that I would be frequenting this building!

When we first arrived and were touring the new camp everything thrilled me. Had I known the English word 'Wow!' at that time, I'm sure I would have said it over and over!

We were assigned a number to look for in the last building they took us to, and were told that would be our apartment. My heart was pounding, and I'm sure I was smiling as I held my children tightly and said to them, "Look where we get to live! This is our new home! We won't sleep on the bare ground anymore!"

I took Punleu to the window and pointed down below and said, "And, look down there, it's a playground where you can play with other children! You're going to make a lot of new friends!"

She smiled at me, and got so excited that she started clapping her hands, and let me know she wanted to go there now!

Oh, how our life was changing! I was in awe to see how excited Punleu was! Life was very sweet indeed!

Paul and Wendy brought us new clothes, pillows and blankets. I looked up to the sky, with tears in my eyes, hoping to see God, so I could thank him in person! It still wasn't clear to me that it wasn't possible here on earth to see God! I couldn't wait to see him, and I had lots of things I wanted to ask him. I had a lot to learn, but I was taking baby steps, learning to walk in a new-found faith. And as I walked toward Him, God supplied me with a new sense of safety, peace and contentment, even though I couldn't see him as I could Buddha. I was excited for what was coming next for us from this God who loved us.

Sorn didn't understand this new wife of his! There was a dimension to my life that he had never known before, and he wasn't at all sure he liked it! By now, it seemed, no matter where we were, we would eventually reconnect physically. But we were at a definite disconnect spiritually, with a wife that believed, and a husband who didn't.

I kept on praying that someday Sorn could understand me, and accept me as a believer in God. Even my friends were of a different sort than I'd ever had before. I surrounded myself with loving Christian friends, friends who opened me up to opportunities. Sorn, however, was stuck in his mind – and though I talked about immigrating to the U.S., he wasn't sure he could take such a risk! He'd needed me to be as I once was, but here I was leading us to Kam-Put Transit Camp. He neither led, nor encouraged me to move forward.

Paul and Wendy came around more often the first month that we moved into the building. I continued working with the Red Cross, teaching the Cambodian language to its personnel.

Paul and Wendy talked to me about the United States, and what to expect when we got there. The areas they covered included, employment, education, business, and transportation - trains, buses, cars, and airplanes. The kind of job one did depended on where he/she lived, in the city or in rural areas.

"It's a land of plenty, Manith," Paul would say, "With supermarkets, and clothing stores galore! Everyone has running water and electricity in their homes!" It was a lot to take in. But I never tired of listening to him and always wanted to hear more.

179

"There are churches, too, where people who believe meet together to study the Bible, just like we do here," they told me. "Church is a good way to become acquainted with the type of people that will be the most helpful, especially when you first get there."

They described the school system, and that attending school was not optional like in Cambodia, but that all children must attend. I thought about my own children, and how they could be educated and would not have to choose between farming and school! (And it also made me remember how I'd suffered in Cambodia because I'd chosen education over farming – how it had put me on a "most wanted LIST" by the communists who felt that education was a threat to communism!)

"But it's a land of law," Paul said, "and you must obey the law. You will have to pay taxes to the government from your earnings. You have to have a driver's license to drive a vehicle. And when driving, you must obey the speed limits, and traffic signs."

I held Paul and Wendy in high esteem. Because they were always talking about God. I thought, no human being is as good and loving as they are. I wondered if they were some of the angels that the Bible talks about.

When I mentioned this to them, they assured me they were very human, but that Jesus was in their hearts, and he helped them to love people and teach them about God. Little by little the truths they taught began to make sense to me. I began to trust in Jesus more than in human beings. Even though I could see humans, and could not see Jesus, I loved and trusted him more than anyone else.

I kept on reading the Bible, and the more I read, the more I understood. However, I had no idea how to become a Christian. I wanted to be just like my mentors, like Paul and Wendy, but I didn't know what faith meant, and I didn't know how a person gave their hearts to the Lord.

I think part of my problem was due to the language barrier. The words they used were mysterious, and even the grammatical differences between our languages influenced how I interpreted what they said. English reversed the order from how you would say it in Cambodian. They kept talking about being saved. I wanted to know what that meant, but didn't know how to ask them. Over and over again they talked to me about confessing my sins to Jesus, and inviting him into my heart to be my Lord and Savior. But all of this seemed strange to me. What were sins? I knew I was pretty good, and not like the communists. What would I confess?

I saw a lot of Paul, Wendy, and Alice in Kam-Put, and I loved to be with them. And then I met Chai, another missionary who was Thai. This little group of friends were not adept in speaking Cambodian, but all of them were attempting to learn it. Whenever we'd be together, they'd want to talk to me in Cambodian to test their language skills.

I started attending some meetings they had with other Cambodian refugees. What I remember about those meetings was how Paul would use the Cambodian Bible, and look up verses that had to do with Jesus. He would very carefully explain, verse by verse, and chapter by chapter, the things that Jesus said and did. Somehow, when I studied in my own language with people that spoke my own language, things started to make more sense! Especially if I attempted to interpret the message for them.

I finally understood this: if I believe that Jesus is real, and that he really died for me on the cross, and that he rose again, and is alive in heaven, then I should tell other people that I believe this. And then I could be baptized to show people I believed in Him. Then I would be called a Christian, because Christians believe what the Bible says about Jesus.

I told the others from Cambodia that I believed, but most of them were still not sure if they believed. They wanted to study more stories from the Bible. They were serious about learning. Others searched for what was true, whether Buddha was the one who they should believe in, or Jesus.

We didn't call it a church, yet, but standing almost in the middle of the camp was a large building built of bamboo logs, with a high roof of bamboo leaves. It was open on all sides. It was provided by the Southern Baptist Organization for the refugees in Kam-Put. Day or night, throughout the week, refugees could enter it to study, sing, and praise the Lord together.

Now that I had pieced it all together in my mind, I told Paul that I wanted to be a Christian. He met with me, and led me to the Lord, and I prayed to receive Jesus Christ into my heart. I surrendered my life to Him.

There was a river running through the refugee camp. The water in the river was so clear and fresh, and sweet to the taste. We used the river water for showers, washing, and cooking, but saved the rainwater for drinking.

I was baptized in that river a week after confessing my faith in Jesus, along with others who had put their faith in Him. I felt set free! With hope in my heart that God would walk with me, I looked forward to the future that God had in store for us.

Chapter Twenty

Sorn's Opposition

*P*aul and Wendy continued to work very hard on processing our application to immigrate to America. They were in contact with the Thai government and the U.S. Embassy constantly. I would normally have been impatient to know all about it, and would have pestered Paul daily to find out 'blow by blow' what was going on. But Jesus gave me a kind of patience and peace I'd never before experienced. I was able to trust God with our future.

And then, Sorn became quarrelsome. He started to resent the time I spent away from him with Paul and Wendy and Christian friends at the church. I would tell myself that my faith is between God and me, and no one can take it away. I wanted to go to church to keep my spirits up, and to feel close to the Lord, but obviously, Sorn didn't understand!

This became very difficult for me. Sorn showed no interest at all in learning about the Lord. I wondered why I'd chosen to reunite with him. All I'd had from him from the time we went to Sisophon was heartache. The crisis in our marriage had to do with culture. Cambodian wives had to bear whatever their husbands did. Mistreatment was expected. Wives went from obeying parents to obeying husbands. They never divorced husbands, no matter what happened, but a husband could leave his wife, or take on other women.

It seemed disloyal of me to share my marriage problems with Paul and Wendy, and I kept it all to myself! Although, I probably should have asked for their counsel. As a new believer, I tried to set priorities for myself: I must put my children first before anything happens to harm them – I am to protect them with my life. I want them to have a better life than I have had.

And I had to consider if a better life for them was possible if I remained married to Sorn. I had not chosen Sorn as a husband, it had been an arranged marriage. I had no option but to go along with my parent's desires. Early in my marriage, Sorn had been physically and emotionally abusive to me. He had lied to me many times in the past, especially about his drinking and gambling, and I had a strong feeling that he would never change. I could not believe a word he said, even now.

It was more for my children that I had submitted the application to the U.S. for asylum, and now, thanks to Paul and Wendy's hard work, the U.S. Embassy in Thailand had approved it.

Though Sorn had addictions and was often abusive to me, I wanted him to succeed. I knew that he was smart and capable, and could do even more than I could when he applied himself.

My foot was not getting better, the infection was still there, and I couldn't be on my feet very long. Perhaps Sorn would help me with my classes, I thought. One day I asked him if he would.

"Sorn," I said, "Do you think you could come to the learning center and volunteer to teach people with me? My foot hurts so bad sometimes, I can't stand up to teach."

I think he needed activity because he promptly agreed to help me. I let the Red Cross Director know that my husband would like to volunteer at the center, and he gave his permission, on my recommendation. Sorn became one of the teachers in the learning center – and that pleased me so much. (I was almost glad for my sore foot!)

I took every opportunity to share with Sorn about my belief in Jesus, and I would read verses from the Bible to him. I feared to say too much, however, or to mention to him about confessing our sins. I knew that would turn him off, for sure. I didn't let him know that I had invited Jesus into my heart, or that I had been baptized. I knew that Cambodian culture dictated that a wife must follow her husband in all things pertaining to religion. If I told him I had converted to Christianity, he would take it as a rebellion to himself.

Sorn once asked me, "Who is this Jesus you keep talking about?"

When I tried to explain, I told him I asked Jesus to forgive my sins, and that he was now in my heart. He thought that was ridiculous and said, "You're crazy. Why do you have to ask Jesus to forgive your sins? What did you do that was so sinful when we were apart?" he wanted to know.

But before I could explain what sin was, he said, "They're brainwashing you, Manith. Tell me who these people are, and I'll tell them to leave you alone."

And from that day on he didn't want to hear anything about my newly found faith. One day he said, "I better not hear you mention Jesus' name again!"

I showed him the Bible that I had been reading for almost two years since I came to live in the refugee camp in Thailand. And I tried to explain to him how it told us the truth about God.

"This is the book that tells me about why Jesus had to die to set us free from everything in the world that makes us do bad things," I told him. "It was Jesus who loved us and who went before us and helped me to escape from Cambodia, and to cross the barbed-wire barrier into Thailand with our children! We're alive today because of him. He saved us from the soldiers who were shooting at us to kill us."

I seemed to have his attention for a while with this, so I went on to tell him, "I trust him, I believe in him completely, I know we're still alive because he is protecting us."

Sorn got very angry then. And started to scold me, "I don't want to see you reading that Bible ever again! I don't ever want to hear you talking to me about Jesus again!"

He told me he knew it was Paul and Wendy and the other people who believed in Jesus and went to that church building that were influencing me, and he threatened to burn my Bibles!

I knew I could not keep on speaking to him about the Lord Jesus. And I stopped trying to persuade him to believe.

I continued growing in my faith, however, and just left Sorn to the Lord. Despite continually being persecuted by Sorn, my joy and hope never faded. I still praised God and thanked Him daily for all he had done and was doing in my life. I knew Sorn's anger could not stop me, or take me and my children out of the hands of Jesus. I secretly read the Bible and kept what I read to myself.

Sorn ended up confronting Paul and Wendy and blamed them for what had happened to me, but they took it calmly and continued their studies with me. I would meet with them at the Red Cross office, and they helped me to pray for Sorn's salvation.

I had lived like a lost soul for so many years, and I never wanted to return to that sad, hopeless life again. I had hope now that Jesus had welcomed me into a walk with Himself, and I knew He would never fail me. He had a plan for my life, and a future already determined for me. I was in a safe place and felt his love.

The prayer times and Bible studies at the Red Cross office continued, and the fellowship with the group of believers and Paul and Wendy kept me growing in the knowledge of Christ. They taught me to deal with my fears, by casting my cares upon Jesus. All of us who studied God's word together prayed together, sometimes with tears, desperately needing Jesus to help us with the trials we were facing!

Paul and Wendy let me know that they thought of me as a daughter, and as a dear Cambodian friend; they were my brother and sister in Christ, and as dear as true siblings!

Every day was so fresh and full of hope, peace, and joy. I felt so much love, encouragement, and support from my Christian friends in the Kam-Put Camp. I continued asking for prayer that the infection in my foot would heal.

The building we worshiped in was very humble, the benches we sat on very hard, but the songs, prayers, and praises that filled it were elegant! We formed a Cambodian choir, and our accompaniment came from a guitar, a violin, and a Congo drum that Paul and Wendy bought for us. The focus of our music was on how much the Lord loved us.

The Bible talks about our "first love" and I knew that kind of love as I used every skill and talent I had to serve the Lord there in the Transit Camp. I loved God and I loved people. Helping and teaching gave me much joy.

Phal Chhith and his wife, Noeurn were special Cambodian friends in Kam-Put Camp, and that is how I will think of them forever. Phal and Noeurn love me like their sister. Noeurn loved to hold my baby boy and sometimes she asked to keep my children overnight at her place, just to love on them. In time my relationship with them resembled the deep friendship I had with Paul and Wendy. I never thought that I could be embraced by such sweet people like these Christians.

Of course, I never forgot my real parents and siblings and still longed to see them someday, hopefully soon, if they were still living.

Paul and Wendy, Phal and Noeurn, others I met with at the Red Cross offices, and my children made my life complete, but for one thing: Sorn.

It was mainly because I had become a Christian that he would never let go of his anger. He reverted to old habits – he started beating me again, controlling me with his physical and emotional abuse.

"I'm putting a stop to all of this," he'd yell, "I forbid you to meet with your Christian friends, or to attend that church any longer!"

I would remain quiet, but in my heart, I knew that I could not stop and that he would not stop trying to make me leave my faith.

"If I ever see you hanging around those people, I'll punish you as you've never been punished before!" he would threaten me.

Sorn didn't believe in any god – and sometimes I think he thought he was God! In Cambodian culture, it was traditional that a woman must worship her husband as her god or idol after she was married. He was to become first in her life, and no god could take his place. There would be no god in the family unless the husband had one that he believed in, and then the wife and children must worship that same god with him. She must focus on her husband at all times, obeying and trusting him in the same way that people obey and trust their gods.

But I couldn't trust Sorn! He had never proven his love to me, just the opposite. His lying, heavy drinking, and gambling made me feel I was only for his use, not someone he wanted to love. When he stole things from my parents, it hurt me and made me feel ashamed! He was not a man of his word, always promising things that he never intended to do. I never knew how to please him, and felt sad that I had seldom thought of him as a loving husband. Sometimes I was convinced he hated me.

And true to who he was, he was continually threatening to harm me if I continued seeing Paul and Wendy and my other Christian friends. I had to lie to him and tell him I was going to the learning center for other reasons when I attended Bible studies. I let my friends know that Sorn was against my faith in Jesus, and anything that had to do with that, and I would ask them to pray for Sorn to have a change of heart!

The year or so that I was alone with my children in Khao-I-Dang was beautiful, but the minute I let Sorn back into my life things changed. It troubled me to lie to Sorn, but no matter what I did, he continued to treat me as someone he hated, rather than someone he loved. To get away from him I would take the children for long walks. As we walked I'd feel set free, but returning, my fears would return and by the time I'd reach our apartment, I'd be frightened to see him again, never knowing what he would do.

This went on for many months and then I discovered I was pregnant again. I didn't know what I would do if the beatings continued! I prayed each night before I went to sleep, asking God to keep me and my children safe. Jesus was my dearest friend. I wept and poured my heart out on the one I knew loved me so much he'd died on the cross for my sins, and he comforted me.

I confessed to Him – the lies and worry and sadness. I'd thank him for saving me, and tell him he was my God, and that I would never put my faith in another! I continued asking him to take my heart and help me in my marriage. I was hungry for His Word, but could only read it when Sorn was not around or I found my way clear to attend a Bible Study. When my troubled husband screamed or yelled at me, I would quietly praise God that Jesus was with me!

After learning I was expecting a baby, I couldn't stand up to everything without having support and I began to share my marriage problems with my Christian friends. It helped me to know they were praying for me, and pleading for my children's father to come to know Christ.

One day I came home from the learning center and saw that Sorn had thrown my English Bible into the fire pit, and it was burned to ashes! I looked at him, broken-hearted, and called out, "Why?"

"I am your god! That book and those friends are taking you away from me!" he yelled in answer to my question.

Sorn did everything in his power to enforce his word. He made sure I didn't go to the church. If I started to sing, he'd tell me to stop! "No more of that silly praising or praying to that foreign god of yours," he'd command.

But when he said I could not speak to my Christian friends, including Paul and Wendy, I spoke up to him.

"They are the only family I have now. We are going to need all the support we can get when our fourth baby is born. They are the reason we have this nice apartment, and the approval to migrate to the United States. Don't you understand that?"

For this little minute I had his attention and I went on, "All the things we suffered in Cambodia, and all the things we went through should have destroyed us – we should have been killed, or died of want and hunger. But God kept them from finding out who we were – people from THE LIST! He brought us here and is giving us a new start. I don't want my children to ever be without the knowledge that there is a God who loves people, and provides for them."

For once he was listening, and I went on, "All of the documents having to do with the Thai government and the U.S. Embassy, were done in just my name, and my children's names. I had them add your name, and yet you treat me like this! I'm a better wife to you now that I know the true God. I've been kind to you, can't you see that? Only God could have gotten us this far."

He seemed to be trying to take in what I was saying, and I think he saw that my faith in Jesus was strong, and had to admit we were living a blessed life compared with how we'd lived in Cambodia. And finally, I think it registered in his mind that not he, nor anything else could keep me from believing in Jesus.

Though there was somewhat of a truce for a short while, living with Sorn was still very hard.

My prayers went like this: Why did you bring Sorn back into my life? Why did you cause us to reunite here in this refugee camp? Won't you please take him away from me?

But then the Holy Spirit would talk to my heart and I could hear him say words I knew were true because I'd read them in the Bible: God is a loving God and full of grace and mercy. It's not his will that any should perish. He always forgives sinners. He died on the cross to save you, but he also died for Sorn.

And then I would get down on my knees and tell the Lord, I will try to keep loving Sorn. I thank you that even though he burned my English Bible, I still have my old Cambodian Bible. I will read it when he is not around, and learn from it, and meditate on what it tells me. But if Sorn will not follow you, please take me away from him.

Whenever I thought about my Bible in flames and burning to ashes, the anger would return, and then I'd know that being angry wouldn't accomplish anything. And I knew deep down that the Lord understood, and I felt his comfort. I already had so much of the Word in my heart, and I knew that the Lord would help me to learn more – he hadn't forgotten me – he was still with me, even if my Bible wasn't! He was looking out for me, and he would provide what I needed!

And sure enough! One day Paul and Wendy brought a new English Bible and a new Cambodian Bible, too, and placed them in my hands.

I took them home and hid them from Sorn. I found a space between the walls of the apartment, where they fit perfectly. And I would take them out and read them when Sorn was away.

One day we had a hard rain. I didn't dare take my Bibles from the wall until Sorn went away, and when I took them out I saw that the water had gotten into the walls. Some of the pages were ruined! But, I could still read parts of it.

God's Word was like a letter from God that I treasured. Every word was precious and valuable. I was so sad that Sorn's heart was still hardened, and that he didn't try to understand my faith. What a different man he would become if he believed, and how much happier our home would be if he knew the Lord.

Each morning as soon as I woke up, my heart would connect with God's heart. I'd tell him, many pages aren't readable in my Bible, but I thank you that many pages can be read and that I will find your messages for me, those that I need for this day. Thank you, Lord.

I found that comparing English verses with Cambodian verses was still the best way for me to study the Bible. And the more consistently I read, the more my faith and hope grew. I still met secretly with Paul and Wendy, and Bong Phal and his wife, which always encouraged me.

Our fourth child 'Sineat' was born in the Kam-Put Camp. She was a tiny and beautiful little angel. I fell in love with her immediately, and she was the light of our world, with a brother and sister who smiled whenever they saw her. As with each of my four children, I would say our family wouldn't be complete without them! In these moments I caught myself thanking the Lord that my family was intact: father, mother, and three children – all together!

Our children bonded very well with each other. Punleu and Kamol adored their baby sister who was a healthy and happy baby. I was in awe and amazed at the goodness of God, who had preserved our lives when we escaped from the darkness of Cambodia, and had placed us in the tender care of the Red Cross, and most of all had brought people into my life that could introduce me to Jesus!

Paul and Wendy stopped by when our little Sineat was born. They brought so much stuff for all of us: fruit baskets, bread, snacks, and lots of newborn baby clothes and things. They told us that they would help us add Sineat to our family list and would resubmit it for acceptance from the U.S. government

After she was born, everything started moving fast. The arrival of a new baby seemed to soften Sorn's heart somewhat. He joined me in thanking Paul and Wendy for what they were doing for us. Sorn and I continued teaching at the learning center. He let me attend church with all three of our children, and it was wonderful to get together again with Christian friends. The only thing lacking was having Sorn join us.

The Cambodian couple, Phal and Noeurn, continued to treat me as their own family. One day Phal said, "I think of you as a sister, and I will always feel that way about you. Both here, and later when we are in the United States, I will find you and help you, and be there for anything you need."

I was overcome with love for him and his wife, and since that day, I have thought of them as my own family. I still knew nothing about my own family, whether they lived or died! It was as though God had supplied an interim family for me!

I loved seeing their children playing with my children on the playground. Like all children, they'd have their little spats, cry a bit, and then start playing again as if nothing had happened! And when I was able to go back to teaching at the learning center Noeurn volunteered to babysit Sineat.

Paul and Wendy knew how Sorn felt about them, and they didn't press themselves on him but kept praying for his salvation. They enjoyed all my children and Sineat got passed around by all of my Christian friends!

One night after I had put the children to sleep, I crawled into bed beside Sorn and had just gotten to sleep when I heard a knock on the door. It was Paul and Wendy. I saw a sheet of paper in Paul's hand and Wendy held a flashlight in hers.

From the light of Wendy's flashlight on the paper, I saw the seal of the United States of America.

Paul smiled and said, "Manith, whose name is on this paper?"

"Mine," I whispered.

"That's right!" he said, "And there's no time to lose! This official letter says that you have been approved to immigrate to the United States of America."

He let that register, and then, continued, "You have to be ready to leave the Transit Camp in two days. A bus will come to pick your family up and take you to the Bangkok airport."

Wendy chimed in with, "We were so happy to get it, and couldn't wait until morning to let you know the good news!

I was speechless. I didn't know what to say! They left and I went back to bed, woke Sorn, and told him the good news; we talked until it was light enough to get up.

The next morning, we went to the Learning Center as usual to teach. We shared the news with our friends at the Red Cross, and of course, with Phal and Noeurn. They were all so happy for us and we all started to pray. Phal was a Bible teacher for the Transit Camp. He was sad to see me go, but he and his wife were very happy to know that my family would leave Bangkok the next morning for America. They came to our place to help us pack and prepare to leave. Phal and Noeurn's children were very close to ours and they were going to miss being playmates.

All of our friends watched us board the bus, and we could tell by their faces that they were already missing us! We waved goodbye – and suddenly, as we drove out of the Transit Camp, we turned over a new page for our lives. The last thing Phal said to me was, "No matter what happens, Noeurn and I will find you again."

They, too, had sent their application to America, and knew that one day they'd hear a knock on their door in the middle of the night, with news that they had been accepted!

Paul and Wendy had driven ahead of us to the Bangkok International Airport to be on hand to help us, and to say their last goodbyes.

We had to show our permit papers from the United States at the Immigration Office at the airport. A security guard then escorted the five of us through the airport to the gate where we would board the plane. I saw Paul and Wendy standing there waiting for us. Punleu and Kamol recognized them and ran toward them. They picked them up and it was plain to us that Paul and Wendy were going to miss our family. "Manith," Paul said with a teasing smile, "We're going to miss your cooking!"

But what I would miss, I told them, would be praying and singing with them, and joining with the Bible Study group.

"You will find good churches in America, so keep on worshiping the Lord. And above all, don't stop reading your Bible – that is what will keep you connected with the Lord," Paul said.

"We'll be praying for you and your family," Wendy joined in, "and asking God to give you a safe trip! We don't know yet where the government will place you, but wherever it is, God will go before and find you a place to live and a place to worship him. Keep the Faith!"

I loved it when they promised to look us up when they returned to the U.S. I loved Paul and Wendy so much! I was so thankful to God for them, that he had put them into my life and that they had led me to know Christ as my Lord and Savior.

The only troubling thought I had was for Sorn. I tried to hold fast to the hope that one day he would see who God was, and that the God who had brought us back together again, would one day bring us together in Christ! But I had a hard time believing that!

Chapter Twenty-One

Journey to America

From the time Sorn joined us at the refugee camp in Thailand, my marriage was a continual struggle for me – the emotional and physical abuse I'd suffered in Cambodia picked up again in the refugee camps. It began in Khao-I-Dang, and when we transferred to Kam-Put it intensified. Sorn began to use both physical mistreatment and threats to control me. Every day was a challenge! Were it not for my new, growing relationship with God, I'm not sure I could have hung on as long as I did. I knew that God would never let me down!

I thought about all of this as the time drew nearer for our departure to the United States of America. My hope was that we would grow closer as a couple in a new country. I wanted so much for our family to remain together. I kept praying for Sorn and for our children to find out who Jesus was just like I did.

I knew that my foot was growing worse and I prayed every day that when we reached America I would find help for it. That was one of the reasons I could hardly wait until we left. When the day finally came, I was eager and reluctant at the same time – fear of flying was something I'd never had before, of course, but I had it now!

The only airplanes I'd ever seen were high up in the sky!

It was November 2, 1980 - and here I was still alive with my name *on another list* – not to be killed, but to find asylum and to *resume life* in a new country! All buckled into a seat on an airplane about to take off from Bangkok, Thailand, leaving for the United States of America – I was full of hope!

Nothing about the inside of the plane missed my attention! It amazed me that something as big as a house could stay up in the sky. There were bathrooms, and a kitchen, and even servants dressed in uniforms! They were continually walking up and down the isles, helping people store their bags above the seats, and serving food and drinks. How heavy it must be with all these people aboard! *What if the plane was too heavy to lift off?*

There were refugees from several different countries, and we were divided up by languages. Sorn and I were chosen to translate for the Cambodians in our section of the plane. Others translated for the Vietnamese and Laos passengers.

What I remember about take-off, was how smooth it was. You could hardly feel it when the plane lifted off. I realized that we were in the air, but I didn't feel any movement in the plane at all. The higher it went, the smaller the things on the ground grew. And soon we were over water. We flew over islands and parts of continents, and the pilot would let us know over the loudspeaker where we were. "You are now flying over the Atlantic Ocean," he announced at our first glimpse of water below. "The entire trip will take approximately 18 hours."

Unbelievable, I thought after translating this for the Cambodians, it took us much longer than that to walk from Sisophon to the Thai border! When we escaped from Cambodia, there were no oceans to cross, but it actually took us longer to reach the border of Thailand, walking, than it was going to take us to reach the United States, halfway across the world by plane.

And I was pretty sure there would be no barbed wire to jump through once we got there! Red tape, maybe, but not gunshots and landmines.

"In our flight from Thailand to the U.S. the plane will make stops to refuel," the pilot announced. "The first stop will be in Japan, and we will be on the ground for one hour." Sorn translated this for the Cambodians aboard.

The 18-hour trip was so well-planned. When we finally landed in San Francisco, California, we were separated into groups, according to our final destinations. Our family boarded a connecting flight to Corpus Christi in the state of Texas.

I was so travel-weary by this time that I could hardly find the right words in Cambodian to translate the flight attendant's first announcement, but Sorn had fallen asleep as soon as we boarded, so it fell to me let the Cambodians know how long we'd be in the air. "We will land in Corpus Christi in two and a half hours," I told them.

No one had thought to tell us about jet lag, but that is what we were experiencing as we walked off the plane at the Corpus Christi airport! I lost my balance walking down the steps they'd rolled up at the side of the plane and was very light-headed, confused, and sleepy. It was cold and windy outside as we walked toward the airport. The wind chill made my nose and ears feel frozen. The sun was brightly shining, but didn't seem to have any heat with it! With every gust of wind, tumbleweeds flew through the air, up and down the airstrip. This is nothing like home, I thought, I've never seen or felt anything like this in Cambodia or Thailand!

It was a bit frightening to see so many people, men, and women, in uniforms everywhere you looked. I thought, they must be employees of the airport. Hopefully, they're not soldiers!

Bewildered, we just stood there – but soon some civilian people walked toward us as though we were old friends. "Welcome to The United States of America!" they said.

They had big smiles on their faces and were stretching out their hands to shake ours. I was so glad I knew what they were saying, and I answered in English, "Thank you." They helped us carry our things from the plane and we walked to a big van, and left the airport.

After a thirty-minute ride, we pulled into a gated community. There were quite a few buildings in this facility. There were people mingling about and they all looked as though they came from different spots of the globe. As our van pulled into the parking lot, we refugees were welcomed by some of the facility personnel.

What a surprise when a man spoke to us in Cambodian. He was easy to understand and we felt truly welcomed, then. He looked over our paperwork: country of origin, medical records, our names, dates of birth, and checked to see that everything matched the records he held in his hands. They did!

He took us into one of the large buildings, down a hall, and into a small room that would be our home while at the facility. It had four beds and a small kitchen. Other family rooms were down the hall from us, and to the left of our room was a bathroom, and to the right a laundry room.

Who would have thought that sleeping on a soft warm bed would be difficult? But it was! We had been sleeping on the hard ground since arriving in the refugee camp. For the first couple of weeks at this new apartment, I slept on the floor, preferring it to the soft bed provided for us. We had so many new things to adjust to!

Our guide took us to a room that was quite large, and let us know it was the community room, where any of the residents were welcome at any time of day. On one wall was a telephone that we could use. There was a large television on another for watching movies and news. And books and games lined up on shelves for all age groups.

"The other people in the facility are just like you, newly arrived to the U.S. You will meet some of them when you come into the community room, and you can help each other, while you adjust to your new surroundings," he told us.

"Come with me and I'll give you a tour of the facility." And, tired as we were, wondering how much we'd even remember, we followed him.

He took us outdoors and pointed at the ocean. "Since we're so close to the ocean, you may see some boats, and fishermen coming ashore. But please don't try to leave the compound, because the guards at the gates will not allow you to leave."

When we went by the play ground, he said, "Corpus Christi is very windy, and a lot of times the winds are very strong. Therefore, we recommend you don't let your children play on the playground without supervision." And then, with a smile, he said, "They could get caught up in a tumbleweed ball and take off!"

We weren't sure if he really meant that – but were taking no chances! Seeing the tumbleweeds rolling about as they had on the airstrip, we thought, we're not going to risk our children being on the playground alone!

My foot was hurting so badly I could hardly walk. But I didn't know who was in charge of medical assistance, and so I decided to just tough it out!

He took us into another room where people wearing uniforms were giving out clothing, shoes, and other things. We could see lots of puffy, jackets along one wall, and along another wall, shoes of every kind and size! In yet another area, regular clothing of all sizes, pots and pans, and other kitchen supplies for eating and cooking.

One of the ladies in uniform came over to us and offered to help us. (Later, we learned about the Salvation Army, and how they volunteered to serve at the refugee center – thus, the uniforms.) "Because you came in the month of October, you're going to need some warm clothing when you go outside. No doubt you've already discovered it's cold and windy in Corpus Christi, even when the sun's out."

She looked us over, sized us up, and brought jackets and coats to us that she thought might fit us. It was a strange feeling to put such clothing on our bodies. In Cambodia and Thailand, it's so warm, that we'd never before had to wear anything resembling coats. We looked at each other and laughed at what we saw! Not only were the coats big and puffy, so were we! But we had to admit, they felt really warm and nice! From Sorn to Sineat, the tiniest little member of our family, we were all outfitted for winter weather! Punleu and Kamol laughed and they didn't want to take their cozy, puffy coats off!

These people were so generous. When we tried on the shoes, they urged us to get several pairs each!

When we'd filled out the application for what we would need, we were asked what kind of shoes we preferred, but we didn't recognize what was meant by the different names of footwear! (What's a boot? what's a sandal? we'd asked each other.) I certainly didn't know the term for flip-flops, but when I saw them in the shoe section, I was so happy. I wondered what they'd been called on the application!

We went back to our room with our arms full! Clothes, coats, bedding, blankets, pillows, shoes, and even things to set up our kitchen for cooking. We couldn't believe it!

But I kept worrying about my foot. I found the manager of the facility and told him about the pain I was experiencing, and he helped me to fill out a request to see a doctor. But, as it turned out, we left the facility before the appointment date came up.

When I asked where I would find rice, fresh meat, and fresh fruits and vegetables, someone who had been at the facility for a while told me that we were allowed to shop for groceries only once a week. "Start making a list, and when the government people take us shopping, you can look for those things at the market."

Market meant one thing to me, but something else to the people we talked to. "Can you find everything in one place," I asked?

"Oh, yes, and more than you can imagine," they answered!

The following week, we got into a big van which drove us to what they called the supermarket.

I enjoyed the ride. We traveled on a road that went alongside the ocean and I saw many fishing boats. On the other side of the road were farms, one after another. Our driver tried to tell us about Corpus Christi, where we now lived. And as he talked, we watched the scenery, only half understanding what he was saying. The people in the fields were being battered by the heavy winds, and I wondered how they were able to get anything done!

Tumbleweeds rolled across the road in front of the van and we almost had an accident when one hit the windshield. It was cold, and I felt like I did at harvest time in my own country. I tried to discover what they were growing, but none of the farms looked like the rice fields in Cambodia, and I couldn't tell what their crops were. And when I asked, I was told, "The things they grow include sorghum, hay, corn, wheat, watermelons, peaches, and pecans."

That's when I realized how deficient I was in some areas of the English language – I recognized none of the names of the crops they'd mentioned!

As the van pulled into a giant parking lot, it was a sea of cars of many colors, interspersed with white ones like the foam of the sea! The cars were all new, clean, and painted in many hues! There were few vehicles in my country, and those I had seen were dull in color and very rarely new.

People walked in and out from a huge building, and I wondered where the market was? They were pushing carts with wheels just full of bags. When they reached their cars, they'd open the trunks, load the bags, and drive off, leaving their carts behind!

And then, we were ushered into the building. I didn't see fresh fruits and vegetables, just shelves and racks everywhere with who-knew-what! We took one of the carts, and looked at the pictures on boxes and cans for things we might recognize and want to buy, but saw nothing that resembled the foods we were used to. We came to a place where there were cases and cases of frozen foods, and we looked and looked before we came to the fresh produce section!

We looked the fruits over, and none of them looked fully ripe! And most were types of fruit we'd never seen before. We looked for our favorites: dragon fruit (hacknoomane), jack fruit (khnor), and rambutan (makhuth) – nowhere to be seen!

The vegetables were in plastic bags, and we wondered how fresh they were and what most of them were used for. They were all so hard!

When we reached the section where there was meat, we whispered to each other, "Does it look fresh to you? Some of it looks like it's been dead for a long time!"

Suspicious is the word that comes to mind! Dare we eat any of it, I wondered, without getting sick? I was afraid to touch any of the stuff in the entire store. I observed and wondered what I should do with all of these things?

I looked into the carts of other people to see what they were buying but didn't recognize hardly anything I knew about.

We watched the people checking out, and saw them rolling everything over a spot on the counter, and wondered what that was all about. I didn't understand how this supermarket system worked. The people buying weren't talking to the people taking their money, and I wondered why the buyers were not trying to get them to sell it cheaper. That's no way to make the most of your money, I thought!

And who was the person taking the money? And then it dawned on me: We had no money! Everything in this market was strange, and frankly, we were afraid to eat almost anything that was sold there!

The only things I had written on my list were: rice, chicken, and vegetables.

Someone came over to us from the facility and said, "Do you want some help?"

"Please." I said.

He not only knew his way around, but he also knew how everything worked!

"We don't have anything in our cart, because we don't have any money," we told him quietly.

"This first time," he said, "the facility pays for your groceries! So, let's go fill your cart."

He led us to the isle with rice. We saw small bags of rice of many kinds, but none like that rice we were used to! There were also little boxes of rice that said: Uncle Ben's Rice. And I wondered who Uncle Ben was! I asked the person helping us if there was any Cambodian or Thailand rice, and he said he didn't think so but didn't know for sure where any of it came from. "Aren't there any bigger bags?" I asked him.

He finally talked us in to buy several small bags!

Once the rice dilemma was solved to the best of his ability, we asked our guide to take us to the meat section.

"Where are the live chickens?" I asked.

"Oh, they don't sell live chickens or any other type of live animals," he chuckled. "Just what you see here in packages.

"How long have they been dead?" I whispered.

"The meat was killed and well-preserved for a certain period of time, and that's why the meat must stay in the freezer or refrigerators until their expiration dates," he told us and saw that we had no idea what expiration meant. "Look," and he pointed to the date on a package, and read it to us.

"You can trust the people that put the dates on the meat, and you won't get sick from eating these meats, as long as you keep them in the refrigerator," he assured us!

I thought, if I want to feed my family, it looks like I will have to trust this strange system they have in this new country, no matter how long the meat has been dead!

The person helping us persuaded us to buy what he considered 'staples,' foods that keep for long periods of time without refrigeration. "That way, when you run out of fresh things, you can eat these until you go to the supermarket again," he told us.

And he placed into the cart things that I had never eaten before, nor knew how to prepare - potatoes, dried beans, canned meats, fruit, juices, and even milk. "Oh look, here's the breakfast food," he said. "Your kids will love this!" And he topped off the cart with box after box of different kinds of cereals and bread.

When we checked out, we'd been informed correctly, the government paid the bill.

I'm not going to complain about the food, I told myself. I must be willing to try new things and learn more about American customs, including its food and everything else. The government is paying for everything – I must be grateful.

I had so much to learn in this brand-new world. It will help if I leave Cambodia behind, its culture and customs, I told myself! After all, this country had opened its arms to people like us whose countries have been crushed by communism.

It was hard, though, not to compare my old country with this new one. America had developed into a country with inventions and technologies that would be beneficial for my children. I would always remember Cambodia as it once was with fondness, but my children would never know that country. Produce for me was tastier and fresher where I grew up, having a part in the planting and harvesting of food. But soon my children would acquire a taste for the foods of their new country – boxed, canned, and covered with plastic.

I would always remember grandmother calling good morning to people walking by and sharing with them, and they with her! But my children would integrate into life in neighborhoods where the people stayed to themselves, and remained, for the most part, impersonal.

The things I must learn and do for the first time, my children would take for granted. I must learn to drive a car – and in traffic which was terrifying! I would have to learn to wash our clothes in a machine! And dry them in a dryer. I would look at the electric stove with knobs and dials I knew nothing about, and wonder how I would use it to prepare food for my family!

Only a plain, ordinary person like myself, from a country like mine, would have been so in awe by her first time in a supermarket. My children would shop in half the time when they became adults! And a small bag of whatever kind of rice would please them just fine!

The first time I washed our clothes in a washing machine, I stood right next to it and watched the clothes going around and around, thinking, it will be a miracle if they're clean when I take them out. I'd put only a cup of what they called *detergent* in the machine, and I was sure that little bit couldn't clean anything!

It amazed me that, without me doing anything, the machine spun the soapy water out, let rinse-water in, and then, in just a few minutes that water drained out! I thought I would at least have to wring the clothes before putting them into the drier, but no! I took them out and they were already wrung – and the clothes were clean, I could tell. I smelled them, and they smelled good!

"The next step," the person explaining things to me said, "is to put them in the dryer."

The machine started to tumble the clothes and kept going in circles until the clothes were dry.

I took the clothes out of the dryer when it stopped. I inspected them! Not only were they clean, but they were also perfectly dry, and looked like they'd been ironed!

These Americans with their amazing technology, I told myself, *have thought of something that frees their people up to do other things while the machines take care of the washing!*

(I had to admit, however, that washing clothes in the river and hanging them out to dry on the line in the backyard, despite the time it took, was something I loved doing! I'd think of each of my loved ones as I handled their clothing, and looked forward to seeing each one all dressed up in what I'd washed for them!)

The next amazing invention I would learn about was the vacuum cleaner. You plugged the cord into the outlet in the wall and turned it on, and it sucked up all the dust and crumbs! They explained that we'd generally get by with vacuuming once a week! How modern I am now, I thought, and I'll never have to make brooms out of straw again to sweep lightly over the dirt, or bamboo floors with the cracks in between!

Punleu loved turning the light switch on and off, and I knew that running through her little mind was: what else is there out there that I can try out in this new country!

The people at the facility dedicated themselves to teaching and training each family about how to live in the United States of America. Each day we learned new things. And I would wonder how we were going to remember it all!

We made friends of some of the fishermen who passed by the facility, and they offered us some of their catches of crabs and lobsters. We enjoyed their visits and loved trying out our English on them. They loved to teach us things, too. They showed us American money and what it looked like, and let us count it, explaining how many pennies how many dimes, how many nickels, and how many quarters made a dollar! I think these fishermen got a kick out of teaching us as much as we enjoyed interacting with them! We'd sit and wait for them to come by!

In time, I heard that we did not have to remain at the Corpus Christi Refugee Camp if we could find someone to sponsor us. They told me that if I found sponsors, I would have to write a letter to the INS in Washington D.C. so they could approve the person who volunteered to sponsor me. (When I wrote down the address, I can remember wondering, what do the initials D.C. stand for? And what does INS stand for?)

Some of the former refugees, who had come to the United States five, ten, or twenty years before, would come to the facility to visit the new arrivals. Generally, they came to see if any of their own family members had arrived, but others came just to visit. Some of them would request permission to take us to meet their families.

They had become citizens and lived like Americans now. They had jobs, homes, cars, and businesses. They were bilingual, and it helped us so much to have them answer our questions about living in the States. Some of the new arrivals were fortunate to be adopted by these former refugees.

I was sitting outside the front door, enjoying a hot, sunny day when a woman asked me, "How long will you be here?"

I told her, "I don't know. Probably until the government finds jobs for us."

"I will be leaving the facility soon to live with my friend in Dallas," she volunteered.

I shared with her that I, too, had a friend in Dallas who had come to the United States as an exchange student before Cambodia was captured by the communists. "I heard that her parents came to America and are living in Dallas, also," I told her.

One day, the same woman and I were in the kitchen, cooking.

"I may have some good news for you about your friend's parents who lived in Dallas," she confided, smiling.

"Do you know them?"

"Of course," she said. "They're coming tomorrow to pick me up! It turns out that we were talking about the same people the other day! And when I mentioned your name to them, they said they knew you! I'm going to be living with them."

I was so excited to meet my friend's parents and I hoped that they would remember me. I knew I looked different now than when I went to high school with their daughter A-Pichh!

Had I sent my papers earlier, I might also have come to the U.S. as an exchange student, I thought, but by the time I sent them, our country was already being persecuted by the communists. Oh, how I hope they still remember me. And, who knows, I might even get to see my old high school friend again!

Chapter Twenty-Two

My Friend A-Pichh

I was so happy that when A-Pichh's parents came to pick up my new friend at the refugee center, they did remember me! We sat down together and reminisced over old times.

"We remember how our daughter used to go to your house to do homework with you," her mother said. "And do you remember that you both participated in the swimming contest in the village, and that my daughter lost the race to you?"

We laughed about that, and I told them, "I'm so glad that you still remember me and all the things your daughter and I did as friends!"

"A-Pichh is married now, and lives in Boulder, Colorado," they told me. "She has a son, and she and her husband have good jobs! We'll give her a call when we get home, and let her know that you and your family have arrived in the States!"

I was so surprised the very next day to get a call from A-Pichh. We talked on the phone for a very long time, rehearsing the good old days in high school, and she told me that I was lucky to have gotten out on Cambodia alive. She asked about my parents, and my siblings. I told her that I had lost all contact with them since my escape to Thailand.

"How did you get to the U.S.?" she asked.

"While I was in the refugee camp in Thailand, I met some Southern Baptist missionaries, Paul and Wendy Williams. They told me so much about life in America and encouraged me to apply for asylum. They told me that the president, Ronald Reagan, had opened the U.S. to refugees of countries that had been taken over by communism. The Williams got the applications I needed to fill out and helped me every step of the way. And here I am – at a Refugee Camp in Corpus Christi, Texas, with my husband and three children."

"There's a lot to learn about the customs and culture in the U.S.A. – and that takes a while," she told me. "Do you like Corpus Christi?"

"No!" I told her! "I'm only 98 pounds, and some days it's so windy here that I think I'll be blown away."

I made her laugh when I said, "I can just see it now. My husband and children chasing after me, rolling along in a mass of tumbleweeds!"

"I'd like to see your husband and your three children," she told me.

"I don't want to lose track of you, Manith," said A-Pichh. "I'll call you every day to see how you're doing."

She kept her promise, and called every day.

A lot happened our first week in the U.S.A.! If I were to itemize all we learned during that week, the list would be long – but the learning was pure joy, not hard at all! Not a bit like the years leading up to this first week! Every day I thanked God for being in this country! No more worrying about being on the communist list

– of being found out and killed! No more wondering what to eat – and finding nothing, chewing on tree leaves. No more running from the enemy, sick, with no one to care or to help, all alone and coming upon pit after pit of those who didn't make it! No more wondering where I could sleep, with nothing to cover me from the cold of the night. No more smells of death and decay!

I was constantly thanking God that the Lord Jesus was in my heart. I knew that these new blessings all came from Him. I kept reminding myself to keep on reading his Word.

I was thankful for a government that had taken us in and given us shelter in this comfortable place. Most of all, though, I was thankful that I had my family with me – all but little Kechara, who was safe in my heart with Jesus.

My faith never went away, in fact it kept growing, despite Sorn's opposition to it. I prayed that I would have a chance to see Paul and Wendy again; I wanted to share with them the good news about my friend in Boulder, Colorado. I prayed to God each night that He would provide a way for me to see that friend in real life. And God was about to answer both of these prayers!

In my Bible I read that God never leaves or forsakes his children, and that He hears and answers their prayers. And I was about to find out it was true!

"Manith," someone called from the community room, "You have a telephone call."

I wiped my hands, smoothed my hair, and hurried down the hall.

"Hello," I answered.

"Manith, it's A-Pichh, how are you?"

"I'm fine. How are you?"

"Do you want to move out of Corpus Christi, before you get blown away?" my friend teased.

"Where would I move to?" I asked, chuckling.

"How about to Boulder, Colorado?" she asked? "Do you want to come live here with me?"

"What?"

"Really. We talked it over and we'd like to sponsor you and your family," she said. "But first, you'll have to submit some paperwork to the INS (Immigration and Naturalization Service). That's the department of government that will approve your family to move from Corpus Christi. "

We talked for a little longer, and after we hung up, I could hardly wait to run back down the hall and give Sorn our good news! But along with the joy I felt about A-Pichh's invitation, I also began to worry about who would help me with the paperwork for the INS.

Someone knocked on our door, and when I went to open it, I could hardly believe my eyes! There stood Paul and Wendy Williams, with big smiles on their faces. I fell into their arms, and could hardly wait to tell them my good news.

They'd inquired about us, and kept track of where we'd been sent, and as soon as they'd arrived back in the U.S. they looked us up!

As usual, Sorn was cautious, but they were just as diplomatic with him as ever. They greeted him, and played with Punleu and Kamol, and commented on how big they were getting – we'd all gained weight with our new diet in the U.S. and the more stationary kind of life we were leading.

"So, you have sponsors already. How do you know them?" they asked me.

I told them about A-Pichh and how we'd been close friends in high school – and that if things had turned out differently, we would have been exchange students together. But communism and an arranged marriage had changed everything for me, whereas she had been in the U.S. all this time, first as a student, and now as a married woman with a child.

"Do you need some help with the INS stuff?" Paul said, before I could ask.

"I was just going to ask for your help! But you always beat me to it," I smiled my gratitude!

Paul told me he would contact the INS in Washington D.C. right away to find out all he needed to know concerning what information we needed to submit. Hopefully they'll get right back to us!

Step by step, the Lord was opening doors for us. I missed our little church in Thailand at the transit camp, and the believers I worshiped with there. I would have hurried right over to the church to tell them what was happening and they would have rejoiced with me. There was a church nearby the Corpus Christi Refugee Camp, but I didn't want to put any pressures on my family by attending it. We were still adjusting to so much that was new.

Sorn was still not a believer – if he were, we could find a church and worship together, something I longed for. But I knew that if I asked to go to church alone with the children, he would say no, and we would get into a big augment. I felt it wiser to wait on the Lord, worship and read His word on my own. I wanted so much to save my marriage, especially for my children, that they would have a father in our home. I knew that I must trust the Lord to lead me and that he would show me what I should do and keep me safe.

In the mean time, we needed to take advantage of all the things we were being taught in the facility, especially about using machinery like washing machines, dryers, irons, electric stoves. They kept emphasizing that anything run by electricity had the potential to hurt or harm. They also explained many things about personal hygiene that were important in the United States. We learned about dentists, eye doctors, and medical doctors. How to secure appointments. And so much more!

It we were to stay on in Corpus Christi, they told us, we needed to know all we could about this area – the business districts, public transportation, hospitals, emergency rooms. They told us, that even if we found sponsors and moved to other areas of the country, that those were the things to find out about right away.

They urged us to make friends, and to be friendly with others in the facility. To interact and help each other, and learn to enjoy activities together, like going to the grocery stores, or visiting while watching our children play in the playground.

When I mentioned wanting to buy larger bags of rice, one of my new friends had faced the same problem, and showed me where I could purchase rice in 50-pound bags. And it turned out to be cheaper, purchasing in quantity. I learned how to accept dead meat from the packages in grocery stores, and learned that fruit from a can was a quick way to serve it, and that canned corn and green beans, went well with my rice and meat, even though they were new to us.

We had never eaten apples, pears, or oranges, the variety here in the U.S.! Before trying anything new, I'd smell it to see if it was okay to eat. I had seen grapes before, but the grapes here were so large, that I told Sorn, "These American farmers must have good soil, full of nutrients, to grown things so big!" And he would agree. I served the new types of fruit to my family, even though they didn't always like them, so that eventually they could replace the fruits we'd left behind in Asia.

"This is not Cambodia," I'd repeat, over and over, when they'd ask for things that were unavailable in the States.

Sometimes on weekends the fishermen would bring us so many lobsters and crabs we wouldn't have to go to the market to buy meats.

Our children would run around and play with the other children, even those who spoke other languages – and I could tell that language was no problem for children. Soon all of them will be speaking English, and mixing right in with the other children wherever they go, I'd tell myself! When I'd see them laughing with other children, I'd start laughing myself, and realize how at peace I was and happy!

Paul and Wendy came back to visit us at the facility, three days after their first visit. When our children saw them, they ran to them for hugs and kisses. Of course, they had to take a look at what was in the big basket of fruit they always brought us.

"I've got some good news from D.C.," Paul said. "The government has approved your friends in Boulder, and have given their consent for you to leave Corpus Christi next week!"

For once, even Sorn smiled! It was good news for both of us!

Paul handed me the document from the ISN that approved our leaving the refugee facility.

"I let them know about your foot, Manith, and they say you must see a doctor as soon as you get there," Paul said. "So be sure you do it, because you want to stay in good standing with the government, and they will be checking up on that!"

Wendy reminded Paul about the other request from the INS.

"Oh, yes," Paul said. "You won't be able to leave this facility until you call the INS office in Texas, who will then inform the facility that you are free to go."

We took care of that last bit of business, packed our belongings, and let A-Pichh know that we were all packed, and had permission from the government to leave the facility.

Paul and Wendy came 'just in time' over and over again since I met them under the tree in Khao-I-Dang, where I first heard the name of Jesus! It seemed to me that the Lord had put them into my life as guardian angels to watch over me and my family everywhere we went!

As they were driving away from the facility they called out the window of their car: "Take care of the permit to travel, and take care of yourselves. Don't forget to see a doctor about your foot. Keep in touch! We love you and will be praying for you."

Sorn was himself again, and didn't wave back, or show any emotion, despite how kind they'd been, and so ready to help us.

Oh, Lord, please help Sorn to see your love through Paul and Wendy! Please help him to believe in you! I prayed for Sorn, even as I threw goodbye kisses to my guardian angels!

We thought we would fly to Colorado, but A-Pichh and her husband, Som-Ang said, "No! We're driving down to pick you up!"

Soon after our goodbye with the Williams, our sponsors arrived at the facility.

I showed the permission from the INS to the officials at the facility, they signed off on it, and all five of us piled into the back seat of their car, on our way to Boulder, Colorado.

Goodbye, Corpus Christi! Goodbye, Fishermen! Goodbye, tumbling, tumbleweeds! Goodbye, hard-working facilitators who taught us so much!

Two days after all the paperwork was handed to us, we were on our way! I think A-Pichh was as excited to see me in person as I was to see her! She didn't waste any time in getting down to Corpus Christi to pick us up!

We stopped at A-Pichh's parents' home in Dallas and spend the night.

When we left the next morning, A-Pichh's mom handed us a big lunch for our trip, saying, "Food will make the trip go faster for the children!"

My mind switched back to my father, tying Kamol and Punleu to my body, and to my mother and siblings handing me food and water for my trip to the Thai border – my own mother telling me, "Keep nursing Kamol. I've filled Punleu's little pockets with bits of food to keep her busy eating. That will make the trip easier for them!"

A-Pichh had brought a map of the U.S.A. for us to study on the trip north to show us how large the country was compared to Cambodia. She had marked Corpus Christi on it, and also Boulder, and told us that it would take us 12 hours to reach Colorado.

Sorn and I poured over the map. We were going fast in the car over good highway, and yet, it was going to take 12 hours! (It only took us 2 hours walking from our village to the Thailand border in peace time, when my family would go there to buy things for my mother's store when I was a girl!) What amazed us is that they would come all this way, take all this time, to show us this kindness! Their marriage seemed so different than ours. They were always teasing each other and smiling at each other.

"This puzzles me," I said, "it took only 18 hours from Thailand to the U.S., but you say it will take 12 hours to go many less miles."

"Well," Som-Ang said, "that has to do with speed! The plane was going much faster than we are."

"But it didn't feel like we were going as fast in the airplane as we are in the car," I commented – still very puzzled!

"Tell us about the flight home!" they asked.

"When we got on the plane we were grouped by languages, not everyone spoke Cambodian, and few understood English. They chose different ones of us to translate for those that spoke our language. Sorn and I took turns translating for the Cambodians aboard the plane," I told them.

The twelve-hour trip was broken up by stopping here and there for snacks and drinks, and bathroom stops. A-Pichh and Som-Ang took turns driving, and we did a lot of looking, and sleeping, in the back seat!

I was so thankful for a friend that would take such a long trip to pick us up from the refugee facility in Corpus Christi, where we got our first little view of America! But this trip overland to Boulder was giving us a much larger view of the changing landscapes of our new country: tall mountains that scared us as we drove through them, dry desert areas where nothing grew but weeds, grassy plains with cattle grazing, very few rivers, but a lot of streams.

Would we ever have the nerve to drive this fast, I asked myself? Or to drive at all? Will their little boy like our children, and vice versa? How long will we have to live with them before we find jobs and can live by ourselves? Will Sorn open up to them? These and many other questions came to my mind as we twisted and turned on our road to what would become our home? Will it feel like home?

When we reached Boulder, and I saw the majestic Rocky Mountains in the back ground, and realized that we'd be living in the foothills of such beauty, I was in awe! It is nothing like our beloved Cambodia, I thought, but a beautiful place, nonetheless, that we will learn to love! Here we are free! And the only 'list' we are on is with a new government that has granted us asylum from the communists!

We settled into Som-Ang and A-Pichh Sok's home. The Sok's son Vuth was 10, and when he met Kamol, who was about 2, he took him under his wings! He brought out his large collection of hot wheels, and sat down on the floor and much to Kamol's joy, he played with him for hours! Punleu, 5, stood shyly to one side, enjoying seeing them crashing their hot wheels cars into each other!

Sorn asked Som-Ang where he worked, and he told him he was the department manager of Human Resources with Denver Social Services and added, "Since you worked with the government in Cambodia, Sorn, I'm thinking I might be able to get you on where I work."

Sorn and I were really happy to hear that.

A-Pichh said, "Now let's think about you, Manith! You'll need work, too. I manage a retail store, but your English is not strong enough yet to hire you to work there. I think I remember, though, that you are quite a seamstress like your grandmother and your mother. There's probably jobs in that field!"

I tried not to ask too many questions, and concentrated on helping in their home, every way I could. But I knew that our time there was temporary, and the more we learned about independent living the better. And, as my sponsor, A-Pichh had many things she wanted to help me with.

She let me know that life was a lot different in America, and not always easy, at first. I had already encountered some differences in Corpus Christi, but she talked to me about many other differences – many of them were things that Paul and Wendy had talked to me about already in the transit camp in Thailand. But somehow, now that we were actually here, it seemed more real.

"We worked hard in Cambodia," she said, "but life was so much more casual there, and actually, I think we work harder here. In order to support our families, we need good jobs, with good benefits. Probably you and Sorn will both have to work, and find babysitters for your children. We need to find you jobs first, and then an apartment or house."

"What do you mean by benefits?" I asked.

"Doctors and medicines are very expensive here. So, one of you needs a job that has good health insurance for its workers – that's the most important benefit for the time being. With that sore foot of yours, Sorn needs to find work as soon as possible," she said.

"How will he get to work?" I asked.

"There are buses. But they take longer to get where you're going, and they run on schedules. If you miss one, you might have to wait an hour for another," she answered. "Eventually, after you get drivers licenses, you'll probably want to drive, for it's very important to not be late for work."

I looked at her skeptically, and she laughed and said, "Driving is not as hard as it looks!"

"Easy for you to say!"

"We must estimate what your rent, food, and utilities will cost, and then find a job for Sorn that will take care of those expenses. The hard thing is, after you find a job that pays for them you must realize that they will take income tax out of your pay check, and social security payments. That makes it necessary for you to work, too, so that your salaries together will support you."

"Utilities – what are they?"

"Gas, electricity, and water!" she said, "You have to pay for them!"

"Social Security?"

"Well, it's kind of like old-age-insurance! When you're in your 60's you'll get a check from the government each month, the amount based on the number of hours you have worked and how much you have contributed from your wages!"

"It all sounds very confusing. Can we do it?" I asked.

"Of course, you can!"

We saw our first snow in December. What does it look like? I tried to describe it to myself. I think it's like damp, shredded bits of white paper falling from a grey sky. At first just a few pieces, and then many, so many that it quickly covers the whole ground like a blanket of white.

At first we just watched it. And then the urge to touch it came upon us. We put on the puffy coats the Salvation Army had given us in Corpus Christi and went outside. We didn't have mittens, and when we touched it, it was so cold it burned our fingers! Or did it bite them? When we picked up the snow, it melted in our hands. When we looked at it, the little shreds of white paper looked more like tiny hard crystals. Soon we saw our puffy coats covered with it, and the wind was blowing it about – softer, but colder than tumbleweeds!

We went racing back into the house. It had been so cold outside, and we kept our coats on inside – looking like pictures we'd seen of Eskimos! We wondered what kept our sponsor's home so warm, and thought, we'll ask them when they get home from work! When we started sweating, we dared to take off our coats. They called this season winter!

In Cambodia, the coldest it ever gets is about 60 degrees, and it happens only during harvest season. And we thought we were cold there!

When Som-Ang and A-Pichh got home from work, we had our questions ready for them.

"We took the children out to touch the snow," Sorn told Som-Ang. "And when we came back in, we wondered how your house stayed so warm, when it was so cold outside?"

Som-Ang said, "Come on, Sorn, I'll show you the furnace!" And they had a man to man talk about how it ran, and how the temperature you wanted was controlled by a thermostat!

"We were also wondering about how cold it is outside," Sorn said.

"Oh, it varies. It can dip as low as zero, and sometimes get's even colder." And these two educated men began to talk about weather, temperatures, and wildlife and how it was affected during the winter season, and any other topic related to the cold.

We women also had our talk about weather, but it went more like this: "Before I take the children out again, I think I need to buy them something warm for their hands."

"What keeps hands warm are called mittens and gloves." A-Pichh, noticing that these were new words for me, was quick to explain, "Mittens have a place for the thumb, and gloves have places for all the fingers! But you'll get used to the weather after you've been here as long as I have. I was pretty fascinated with snow when I first saw it, and now I know that it is only for the winter season, and not everyday then, and that summer is always just around the corner, and then, you're warm again like in Cambodia. Well, not quite like in Cambodia!"

Vuth spoke up then and said, "Mother, let's make some snow-cones for the children!"

A-Pichh and Vuth put on their coats and came in with some crispy hard snow, and got out some cones and packed them full of snow, and poured some syrup over them, and handed them to Punleu and Kamol! To say it delighted them is putting it mildly!

Chapter Twenty-Three

On Our Own

From the start, Sorn and I were eager to work. We wanted to pay taxes to the government that had been so good to us, and to obey all of its laws. We were learning so much, just by observing our sponsors. We could imitate them, and one day, perhaps have all the things they had.

We got along so well with our friends, they were so gracious and helpful, and we never felt in their way. Som-Ang found Sorn a job as a social worker for the city of Denver. And just as he'd thought, Sorn's college education and his work in Cambodia for the government looked good on his application. His job had good health insurance, and I was finally about to see a foot doctor.

Both the doctor and I were shocked at my first appointment! He, to see a foot in such a condition, and I, to hear, "I can see that you have had an internal infection in that foot for many years, and now you have tetanus! We'll have to amputate your foot!"

He could see the affect this had on me, and went on to explain why the amputation was necessary. "The flesh on the wounded area is starting to fall off and we can almost see the bone. This is a very dangerous thing," Doctor Barns told me, "I cannot guaranty that tetanus won't spread throughout your body, even with the amputation."

"No!" I said. "I refuse to have my foot cut off."

"Okay," he said, shaking his head in disbelief that I would not let him amputate. He gave me a tetanus shot, and said, "We'll put you on antibiotics!"

It took four more years before we saw healing take place, with constant doctor visits, and changes of antibiotic medications! There is still a large callus that forms at the bottom of the original wound – a constant reminder of stepping on a board in a rice field with a rusty nail in it while escaping for my life.

(I thank God that I am able to walk straight today, though once a month I have the callus shaved off so that I can continue to walk comfortably. Though my foot is deformed, I'm so grateful it's still there – and praise the Lord that I made the decision not to let Dr. Barns amputate.)

The map that A-Pichh took along for us when they drove to Texas to pick us up convinced us that America was huge! And later, by studying a map of Colorado, we began to understand how a state has its own entity and its own government, and yet is also a part of a nation comprised of many other states: which explains the nation's name – the United States of America. The federal government has to do with all the States, and each individual state has its own government! And that is why you must pay both federal and state taxes! We learned that each state has a capitol city – and nearby Denver was Colorado's capitol. And the capitol of the whole country was Washington in the District of Columbia. (That's what D.C. means! I exclaimed, when I learned that fact.)

Granted it was all very confusing at first, but gradually it all began to make sense.

We learned that Cambodia is about 1.5 times smaller than Colorado in size. However, its population is larger than Colorado's.

Where Colorado has approximately 5 million people, Cambodia has 11.9 million.

It took me only a month to find my first job, which was working for a woman who had a drapery business. After that, I went to work for a company that made western clothing – like the cowboys in the movies wear.

We became acquainted with another Cambodian family, living close to our first home. We knew we could trust them and hired them to babysit our three children. As soon as we dropped the children off with them, Sorn and I would hop on the bus that took us near to where we worked. That arrangement lasted through the years, even after our children were in school – they were willing to drop our kids off and pick them up after school and keep them until we picked them up after work.

Occasionally A-Pichh or Som-Ang would drive us to work.

We moved out of the Sok's house after a month and moved into an apartment. And after only a year, we were able to save enough money to buy our very first home – not in Boulder, but in Denver, nearer our work. A few months later, we bought our first car. Sorn learned how to drive and got a driver's license and drove to work every day. We were so happy that we didn't have to depend on the generosity of our friends for too long, and we were always grateful for their sponsorship, and hospitality!

Our first home had three bedrooms and a garage for our car. There was a good-sized backyard for our three kids to play in and I could watch them playing together from the kitchen window.

Not only were we happy with our situation, and with our babysitters, we realized we could help Sorn's family who had escaped to Thailand and had arrived in the Koa-I-Dang Refugee camp. The money we sent was a big help to them.

I never gave up my search for my parents and siblings. I felt sure that God was hearing my prayers and that one day I would see that he had answered them. Father, I prayed daily, please bring my family out of Cambodia.

I had news that Paul and Wendy Williams had returned to Thailand and were once again working on the missionary team there. It had been five months, though, since I had heard anything, and I began to worry about what had happened to them. They'd been my mainstay since I'd let Jesus into my heart, and it felt so uncomfortable to have lost all contact with them. I kept writing to them to let them know where we were living but never heard back.

If I brought up my concerns to Sorn, he would yell and become angry.

"I'm glad they've dropped out of your life! I hope we never see them again," he'd tell me.

I couldn't understand why he disliked Paul and Wendy so much! Or, for that matter, any of my Christian friends.

While we lived with the Sok's, Sorn did not abuse me, but once we were living on our own it started up again. I began to feel trapped and feared that one day Sorn would really hurt me. I knew that I could tell A-Pichh about what was happening, and she would help me to figure out what to do, but because of the fear and shame I felt, I kept his abuse to myself.

We had every reason to be a happy family – we had a home, a car, jobs, and our kids were doing well – but we were not happy! Sorn's old habits returned: he started drinking and gambling with some of his Cambodian friends, and the time he spent with them increased every week. If I said anything to him he'd respond, "I'm making the most money I've ever made, and I need to enjoy my life! And hanging out with my friends is how I do that! Just leave me alone, I'll take care of our money and I won't let you go hungry."

I really became concerned when he wouldn't come home from work. He'd come home late at night, saying, "They had some late meetings at work and I had to attend them. Don't worry when I'm late getting home!"

It was the same old story I'd heard before, in Battambong, and again in Sisophon. I didn't question him, even though I knew what he was doing. And we sort of grew apart. I made friends here and there around the city of Denver, through work and through our babysitter. And he did whatever he wanted.

A Cambodian community group had formed in Denver and we were invited to join with them throughout the year whenever they'd get together. The Cambodian New Year's Celebration was the highlight of the year. There were a lot of people in the group, and with each event, we made more and more friends. For Sorn, that meant more people to drink and gamble with. Soon he was coming home only once a week.

Our savings dwindled and sadly he stopped sending money to his family in the refugee camp. If I mentioned his family, he'd lie and say, "Everything has gotten so expensive, we just can't afford to send them money anymore! We need all we can get just to meet the needs of our own family."

He insisted on taking care of our finances himself, and I was left completely out of the loop. I never saw any of our bank statements, because he did all the banking. I would hand my paycheck over to him and had to ask him for any money I needed. I never asked how much we had in the bank in either the regular or savings accounts. But he was always telling me, "Our savings account is very low."

I began to suspect he was taking money from that account for his gambling. I had the chance to ask him about it one day, though I was afraid that he might become violent.

And I was right! I brought the matter up when he got home after being absent for a whole week. He was drunk, and when I asked if he was taking money from our saving account for his drinking and gambling, he hit me and said, "There's your answer!" He warned me never to ask questions about our money again.

He was in the United States, but continued to believe in marriage Cambodian-style: wives do not question their husbands or make any decisions concerning money; they serve and obey their husbands; all friends are chosen by the husband, and all the friends a wife has must be made from among his friends.

I was Cambodian, too, and tried to follow these customs, but it seemed very hard to do in the United States where all the women I knew from work had their own money. I was trapped in a marriage doomed from the start, I felt. I was always making excuses for the bruises on my body that showed, though everyone suspected they came from my husband's abuse! And this shamed me.

In my heart of hearts, I knew that abuse was wrong, but I didn't know how to stop it. I spent the first two years in Denver as a victim – not of communism any longer, but of my own husband! But I still tried to protect Sorn's reputation and hid his cruelty from all our acquaintances.

It usually started at dinnertime. Sorn would find something to disapprove of! And when he got going, his anger knew no bounds! He'd pick up the bowls of food and other plates from the table, and throw them on the floor and at the walls of the kitchen, leaving food splattered everywhere.

Our children would be so frightened, they'd start to cry, and, most of the time, they'd hide in the closets or in the garage. Every time Sorn was around, things got worse, and yet when we'd meet with friends, or someone he knew, Sorn always acted nice and loving to me and the kids.

It was like being married to two different men – the one he was in our home and the other he became when we were outside it! Day and night, I was in emotional turmoil. I wanted to keep the promise I'd made to my parents to be totally committed to the man they'd chosen to be my husband, but, for the sake of my children, I knew I needed to spare them the unhappiness of a home with Sorn in it!

Oh, how I wished I could let Paul and Wendy know some of my marriage's problems. And then one day a letter came from Wendy, explaining why they hadn't been in touch with me.

"I'm sorry to let you know, Manith, that Paul has passed away after a fatal heart attack," she wrote. "He died in his hometown in Hawaii. I knew you'd want to know. Perhaps you can attend his funeral. I'd love to see you if you can come." And then she gave me all the details.

I wrote her right back and told her that I would not be able to attend Paul's funeral because I didn't have money for the flight.

I could not go to her, but Wendy came to me! And while she was with me, I told her what I was going through with Sorn. "What shall I do the next time he hits me?"

I thought she'd probably counsel me to hang in there, and that in time things might get better, but instead, she said, "Manith, there must be no next time! Abuse is something real, and you must not treat it as something you are forced to go through."

She provided me with the phone number for an abuse hotline. "Don't wait till Sorn comes home to abuse you again; call right away, and do whatever they ask you to do. You're not only doing this for yourself, but you're doing it for Sorn and for your children! You are in a very unhealthy marriage."

Wendy looked very sad and tired. I prayed with her before she left for Hawaii. I asked her to be in touch if she could, and she said she would. I wished I could go with her, but I knew I had to be with my family.

She hugged me, and bent down, and hugged each of the children! Her last words to me were: "Take care of your children and I will continue to pray for you!"

"And I will pray for you, too!" I told her.

Chapter Twenty-Four

The Cost of Addiction

I knew that I should have heeded Wendy's advice to call the abuse hotline. I know now that they would have explained to me that I was actually enabling Sorn by hiding what was going on. I would have gotten help for myself, which indirectly would have helped Sorn to face his addictions. But, I didn't, and a few weeks after Wendy left, I faced another conflict with him.

He came home very late at night, full of anger. I woke up, and got up quickly to prepare food for him to eat. He'd lost a lot of money gambling, and I knew that if I didn't do things just right he would take his anger out on me!

"Please don't go gambling tomorrow, Sorn," I begged. "We miss you. Let's take the kids to the park, and visit while we watch them play."

When he finally turned in for the night, he agreed to spend the next day with me and the kids.

The next morning, however, he was already gone when I woke up! I prepared a little picnic lunch, and decided to take the kids to the park by myself – attempting to wash away their father's unkept promises. [

I continued to pray and ask God to help me know what I could do to help Sorn understand that what he was doing was not only bad for him, but also prevented me from giving our children the type of life that was best for them.

What really started me thinking I might have to leave him, was that his abuse was now extending to how he treated our children. Not only did he pick fights with me, he would pick fights with them, yelling at them and threatening to beat them. When this happened, they'd come to me for comfort.

"Sorn," I would tell him, "if you must beat someone let it be me, but leave the children alone!"

When any of the children would run to me, I'd hold them close, and tell them, "You are my whole world! I love you so much. I promise you that I will not let your father hurt you!"

In most ways, I was raising the children alone. Sorn rarely interacted with them, except negatively. I took care of them, fed them, and gave them the love and friendship they needed. They were in school, and I'd help them with their homework, and praise them when they did a good job. The children and I had a healthy relationship – they loved me, and knew that I loved them.

Like my grandmother and my mother before me, I felt that one of the ways a mother shows love for her children is to keep them well-dressed! In all my free time, I sewed!

I gave my pay checks from work to Sorn, but I was doing alterations for people on the side, and I saved those earnings for me and the children, without reporting them to Sorn. And that is how I would buy the materials I needed for the children's clothing.

During the summer I made a big vegetable garden in our backyard which helped us with our food expenses. Because of all the money Sorn had to pay on his gambling debts, he was giving me less and less money for groceries.

Sorn would not allow me to learn how to drive, so I had to depend on the kindness of people from work to drive me to the places I needed to go.

Every payday Sorn would come for my check which he would deposit in the bank, and then turn around and take money out for his costly past time of gambling. He left all the parenting up to me – and even if he was home, and much more qualified than I to help with homework he would send the kids to me. He was convinced that the sole responsibility of a father was to go to work. Playing with his children was not something he participated in, nor did they seem to expect it from him.

I saw how American fathers took their children to the park, and out for treats, and longed for Sorn to notice this also. But I'd always make excuses for him. I'd remind myself, though we live in this country, we're Cambodian not Americans, and Sorn is just being who he is. I promised I would be faithful to him and obey the Cambodian marriage customs! And that I will do!

Sorn was always good at his work, even designing irrigation ditches for the communists. His intelligence and skills got him promotions at the Social Service office, with significant pay raises. I was very proud of him, but I couldn't see our lives getting any better! Our future looked very dim. The gambling and drinking, the violence and abuse continued to tear down our marriage, bit by bit!

I didn't want to feel this way, but my fear of getting hurt every time he lost his temper, made me want to run away with my children. To run away from communist cruelties was something I knew all about, but it seemed such a sad thing to feel like running away from a husband's cruelties.

I felt that Sorn was betraying my trust – preferring to live a life apart from me and our children. Our marriage took a blow each time Sorn lost his temper and laid his blows on me. We'd been in the U.S. for two years, and Wendy was the only one I'd told about the abuse. No one else, except the children, knew what Sorn was like in our home.

My foot was healing, and I could finally walk without pain on my own two feet. I praised the Lord daily for those two feet, and that the tetanus had not spread throughout my body. Most of all, that I had made the decision not to let Dr. Barns amputate my foot.

I wasn't totally without pain, however. Sometimes I had so many bruises all over my body that I could hardly lift my arms to pick up my children; it even hurt to hug them. At work, I would have to pretend I was fine, but even there I would almost cry out when performing my work, the pain would be so severe.

I made excuses for Sorn, so that my children wouldn't think their father was cruel and uncaring. At meal times, when we sat down to eat, they'd miss him, and ask me where he was. I would lie to them and say, "Your daddy had to go out of town for job training," or "he's in meetings."

They were always happy when they would see him coming home. His children loved him and missed him greatly. They felt he was a very important man, because of the stories I would tell them to cover his absences.

I think for a while I half believed the stories myself that I told people about his frequent times away! To admit we had a bad marriage would have brought me shame.

We were into our third year in America when I started dreading the times he would come home – the only thing I could expect were fights and beatings, and added to that, the financial troubles we were in. He was losing so much money now, that he ignored the mortgage payments.

"Do you think I need to get a second job, so we won't lose our house?" I asked one day.

"No, I do not!" he told me sternly. "I don't see why we need to own a home, anyway, it's just a big, unnecessary expense!"

I was forming quite a few friendships at my job, and it was comforting to have good friends to work with. For a little while, with them, I'd stop thinking about how bad things were at home. Many of them were concerned about my bruises, and caught on to the fact that I was married to an abusive husband.

"Manith, you have to get away from him, your life is in danger," they'd tell me. "And not only your life, you're putting your children's lives in danger, too."

This frightened me! But I still wasn't ready to leave my marriage. I prayed to God about it, and hoped things would turn around, and Sorn would stop beating me and become responsible once again.

One stormy night with rain pouring down outdoors, it was just as stormy indoors! Something set him off, and Sorn lost his temper in front of our children while we were eating dinner in the kitchen. He was mad, because some people had pounded on our front door, demanding the money he owed them from gambling! They had shouted and threatened him saying, "You're going to be in big trouble, Sorn, if you don't come up with the money!"

They left, but the threats seemed very real and I was scared! I asked him, "Sorn, how much money do you owe them? How did they know where we lived? Are the kids and I in danger?"

I went on to tell him, "We need to pay the babysitter by the end of the week, and they'll shut the electricity and water off if we wait any longer to pay them!"

That made him so upset that he picked up a bowl full of soup and threw it at me. It hit my head, and blood gushed down my face.

Our kids started to cry, partly to see the blood, and partly to see how angry their father was getting. I got up from my chair and grabbed the children in my arms, and at the same time, grabbed a dish cloth and used it to try to stop the bleeding! Sorn went crazy and started screaming. He kicked me in my back, and slapped my face. "It's all your fault, Manith," he said, "You told those people where we lived and that's how they knew where to come!"

"Sorn, I don't even know them, how could I have told them anything," I tried to reason with him.

But he just shouted back, "It you ever leak to anyone where we live, I'll kill you!"

That was the first time he'd ever threatened to kill me, and I knew for sure that it wasn't an empty threat! I thought, one day I will die at my husband's hands! I have to do something to protect my children! I didn't want my life to end like this. No longer could I convince my children what a fine man their father was – they'd seen him at his worst, and heard his threats on my life!

Sorn took off! I gathered the children into my arms, and told them I would take care of them. I quieted them and tucked them into their beds. I continued to cleanse the wound on my head, desperately needing help, but not knowing who I could turn to. I went to sleep thinking, perhaps Sorn is gone for good!

But three days later in the middle of the night, he came home! "I'm hungry," he announced.

I made him food to eat, hoping it was to his liking so he wouldn't find something to quarrel over. Later the next day, he said, "We have to sell our house, we're too far behind on our payments – it's close to a year now in arrears."

I was shocked; but it made sense, because he has been drinking and gambling for the whole year.

He had kept me in the dark about the seriousness of it all. He had control over our money, his pay checks, and mine, and I'd been told, "Your job is to trust me and ask no questions!"

When I couldn't hide my pain any longer, I started sharing what I was going through with my boss Rena and her husband Harold. They would listen to me, and help me all they could. When Sorn didn't show up to drive me home from work, they'd take me home, and stop by the babysitters to pick up the children. And when it was time to pay the babysitter, if I didn't have the money, they'd pay her.

This made me ashamed that they had to help me so often. I explained how I had to hand my paycheck over to Sorn, and I had no money of my own. I told them that I couldn't ask him for money if he came home drunk, because he would get angry and the abuse would start.

Not only were Rena and Harold my bosses, they were my best friends. I felt that I could trust them much like I had Paul and Wendy. Despite my marriage trials, God was constantly supplying those who could help me – people who brought me blessings and comforts during hard periods of my life when so much was beyond my control.

I felt great shame for Sorn's abuse, and was continually trying to hide it from Harold and Rena. When Rena asked me about bruises she'd noticed one week, I lied and said, "I was dizzy and fell and hit the corner of the bathroom door."

They knew what a sad existence it was for the children and me not to know from one day to another what would happen, and they would surprise us, and ask to take us out to eat when they sensed we were going through times when Sorn was not showing up. When they'd leave us off, they'd say, "Manith, it you need anything, give us a call!" And I knew they meant it.

One day I felt sick after a hard night with Sorn, but I still went to work. I had no sooner entered the building, when I collapsed on the floor and passed out. Rena and Harold took me to the hospital. The doctor informed them after examining me that I had been hit many times on the head, and that the nurse had found more bruises throughout my body, not just those that were in evidence on my face. He wanted me to stay at the hospital for a night for observation, and to make sure I had plenty of rest and nourishment.

Rena and Harold kept my three children with them overnight while I was at the hospital. They dropped us off a bit late at home. I was glad they hadn't come into the house with us, for when we walked in we found Sorn in the kitchen looking for food.

"I'm hungry. Make me some dinner," he said, "and then we'll talk!"

I was so scared to see him and didn't let him know that I had been in the hospital – knowing that he would have gone into another rage if he knew.

After I fed him, I put the children to bed.

"Be ready to move out soon," he told me, without any other information.

"Where are be going to live," I asked. "Do we have enough money for an apartment?"

"I don't know," he said. "I don't know what we're going to do."

"Are you going to stop drinking and gambling?" I asked.

"Yes, I'm going to stop," he assured me. But I knew I couldn't believe him. "Call your bosses tonight and see if they can loan us money."

"No, Sorn," I said, "I can't do that."

That's all it took. When I refused, he started to kick me, and I was already in so much pain, that I cried out so loudly that it woke the kids up and they all came running to me, and did not want to go back to bed.

He slapped me and kicked me toward the kitchen wall. He'd been drinking, and was so drunk he was out of his mind with anger. Punleu, started yelling, "Stop slapping and kicking my mom!"

"I'm going to kill her," he shouted back!

Our son was only four years old but he ran to help me and pleaded with his dad, "Please don't hurt mommy any more!"

Our baby girl Sineat sat right by the door of the bedroom, crying and shivering.

I could see the children were sobbing and so terribly frightened, that I told them, "Let's pray that God will help us. He's always there! He tells us that when two or three of us pray to him, He'll protect us." We tried to ignore Sorn, and began to pray together, but Sorn pulled the kids away from me, and pushed them out of the kitchen.

"Stay away from you mother!" he shouted.

245

As soon as our children were out of the kitchen, the kicking and punching began in serious. When he hit me hard in the chest, blood came out my mouth, and I became so weak I collapsed on the floor! I could hear my oldest daughter talking with 911 on the phone. She was begging them to come quickly, because her father was going to kill her mother.

I woke up in the hospital twenty-eight days later, surrounded by my three precious children, with social service authorities, and some doctors and nurses in the room.

They were all smiling.

"Welcome back! You're awake!" the medical professionals said.

I recognized my children, and held my arms out to them. I held them as tight as I could, happy and comforted to hear and see them.

I had no idea how long I'd been in a coma, and felt as though I was just waking up from a long sleep. "Have you eaten," I asked my kids.

Punleu said, "Yes, mommy, we just ate fried chicken!"

"Fried chicken? Can I have some, please?" I asked them.

The doctor said, "You can eat anything you want after the authorities complete their interviews."

I wondered what was going on, and why the authorities needed to interview me? Did I do something wrong?

Punleu said, "Mommy, we haven't been home for a long time – we've been staying with other people."

"Where's your father?" I asked her.

"I don't know," she said, "We haven't seen him for a long time either."

"Have you been going to school?" I asked. And she said they had.

Then, I felt pain in my back, my neck, my face and legs, but the most painful was my chest. I had a hard time breathing, while I carried on my conversation with my kids. Kamol did not have much to say, but kept holding my hand and smiling. Sineat walked over to me and said, "Mommy, let's go home, you are awake now! You have been sleeping for a long, long time. God saved you because I've been praying for you to wake up."

The last thing I remembered was praying with the children that fateful night when Sorn almost killed me. And it meant so much to know that my precious children had their prayers answered, and that they were with me when I woke up at the hospital.

The social service lady came back into the room and said, "I promise, I will bring them back to you very soon," and she took all three with her out of the room.

One by one the authorities interviewed me, asking a lot of questions. They asked, "Do you know why you are in the hospital? Do you know what happened to you? Do you know who you are? Do you have a family?" And many other questions.

I told the authorities that I didn't want to go home. "I remembered that my husband hit my upper chest so hard blood came out of my mouth. He kicked me in the back, and slapped me around my face and head."

I wasn't sure why I was in the hospital, I told them, and let them know that I had no relatives living in Denver. "The people I work for have been very good to me, and I have a few friends at work," I said.

The authorities ask me if it was okay if they contacted Harold and Rena.

"Yes," I said, "But I don't have their phone number. But this is my work address where you can get in contact with them." And I told them the address.

"We want you to know what happened," the authorities told me. "You were admitted to the hospital twenty-eight days ago, in response to a 911 call that your daughter made. She told them that you had passed out and was lying unconscious on the kitchen floor."

I was so surprised that Punleu had the presence of mind to call 911. Otherwise, I would surely have died.

"You suffered severe trauma to the head and chest," they continued to inform me, "and had so much internal bruising, that it's going to take time to heal your entire body."

The doctor told me that according to the x-ray of my head injuries, I might suffer some memory loss and brain function. "Twenty-eight days is a long time to be in a coma," he said. "We were afraid for a while there that you weren't going to regain consciousness."

I was both frightened by what they told me, and at the same time sad that Sorn was capably of causing me so much damage. Yet, when the authorities asked if I wanted a restraining order put on him, I said, "No." I still held out hope that Sorn would realize what he had done to his family, and turn his life around.

Harold and Rena took the children and I into their home for a couple of months after I was released from the hospital. They would take the children to school, and pick them up and bring them home when school was out. What a blessing it was to have someone looking after us, and not having to fear Sorn coming home. I knew that Harold and Rena loved my children like their own and if anything came up, they'd know what to do.

After three months, I told them I wanted to go back to work again. "I'm sure I'm strong enough now to handle my work," I told them. I rode to and from work with them, and after two more months I felt strong again – healed from all the internal bruising!

I was startled one day when I got off work to see Sorn's car parked in front of the company I worked for. When he got out of his car, I panicked! He spoke and said, "Manith, thank you for not pressing charges against me. I'm still a free man and I want you to come home with me. I still have my job, and I'm going to work every day, and trying to stay clean."

By this time Harold and Rena had joined me, and were witnesses to everything he said. "I've stopped gambling and drinking and am living at our house by myself." He hesitated, and then said, "I'm lonely and I miss you and the children so much."

I didn't go with him right away. Harold and Rena and I had a lot to talk about, weighing the risks against the changes he claimed he'd made, and deciding whether to believe him or not. We decided I would move back and try once again to live together as a family.

I had to prove to myself that he was truly changing. And yet, he kept receiving phone calls and I overheard conversations about him still owing money.

I knew how he was, I knew that he got angry over any suggestions I would give him, and yet I felt I needed to tell it like it was. So, one day I opened up and said, "Sorn, they do counseling at churches and lots of people have been helped by it. I think you should try it."

He wasn't drunk and he hadn't been gambling for a few weeks, but I sensed I was in danger as soon as I finished speaking. "I want you to know," he began, trying to stay calm, "how hurt I am that you think I need to see a counselor!"

I felt the madness in his voice and the change in his attitude. He began to curse and to throw things around. He didn't hit me directly, but I knew with any type of suggestion I might make, the abuse would start all over again. This was no way to live.

One day I saw a couple of middle-aged men knocking on our door. Sorn went outside to talk to them. I realized that after a couple of hours Sorn had gone off with them.

I felt that something was going to happen to me and our children. The rain was pouring down, and I wanted to be gone by the time he got back. I called Harold and Rena to come get us. I packed my children's clothes and my own. When they got there, I said, "I have some Cambodian friends who will put us up," and I told them where to go and they dropped us off at their house, but before driving away, they said, "Call, if you need us!"

I begged my friends to give us temporary shelter, at least for one night. "I just need a place for my children to lay their heads, because it's getting late and it's pouring down rain. And please," I pleaded, "don't let anyone know we're here!"

"We don't want any trouble with Sorn, either, so we'll tell no one!" they told me. "Why don't you just go home?"

I finally told them what had happened to me, and that if I went home, this time Sorn would kill me, and I wouldn't be as lucky as I was when I survived the last abuse and the coma of 28 days.

At last, I knew what I had to do. For love of my children, I would leave our home, so that they would never have to go through seeing me abused by their father again. I may have survived his kicks, slaps and punches, but I knew if he turned on the children, they would not! I was willing to die for them, but I knew that what they needed the most was for their mother to live for them and to take them out of Sorn's hands forever! They had seen enough, and would be marked for life by what I'd put them through for not leaving before this. We're going to get healthy again as a family, I told myself. I must find a way to protect us from Sorn in order for us to live successfully in America.

I hardly slept a wink all night long, brainstorming about how I was going to let my friends know in the morning about the decision I'd made.

It is going to be hard to find the right words to explain what I am about to do to the children, I told myself.

I wasn't sure what I would do, exactly, nor how everything was going to work out, but I knew for certain that I was going to leave Sorn – this time forever. I knew my kids had gone through too much already, and I was determined they'd never go through it again.

When I told them that I was going to find another place for us to live, they asked if their father would be there.

"No, he won't," I said, "without mentioning his abuse as the reason."

They looked relieved and said, "We don't want to see our daddy angry and drunk. He does bad things to you, then!"

I need not have worried about telling them why I wanted us to move, they were already on the same page as myself! I didn't want to see him drinking, angry, and out of control ever again, either. From here on out, I would do all I could to reclaim a normal childhood for them, that Sorn's abuse was robbing them of.

We stayed with my Cambodian friends for three months, and then moved into a two-bedroom apartment. They helped me get settled into the apartment and gave me so many things to furnish it. My kids enrolled in a new school and seemed very pleased with their new environment.

Harold and Rena gave us the money to put down on our new apartment. How blessed we were by the people that God put around us like guardian angels. Each time we sat down at the table to eat, we'd pray and give thanks to the Lord for his provisions and protection. Though having little was hard at times, I found ways to get by, and enjoyed the challenge.

I saved a little from each paycheck for a car. Some day I'll learn to drive and we'll buy a car and I will drive my children and myself everywhere we need to go, I kept telling myself, as my savings account increased little by little – and having my own bank account, no one would gamble it away.

I was still in contact with Wendy. I let her know the children and I were now living on our own, and gave her our new address. It was fun sending her pictures of how big the children had grown. I knew she'd be relieved to hear that Sorn was now out of our lives, something she'd recommended years before when I'd shared his abuse with her.

Harold and Rena came to look over the new apartment they'd helped us get into, and they seemed pleased to see how well we were doing. "Until you get your drivers license and a car, we'll pick you up and bring you back to the apartment every day," they told me.

"And I'll teach you how to drive," Rena said!

The apartment managers, John and Maggie, volunteered to make sure that Punleu and Kamol got on their school bus every morning. "Then, in the afternoon when they get home, they can stay in our office until you get back from work," they told me. Punleu and Kamol loved staying with the managers because of the snacks she'd have ready for them after getting off the bus. We picked Sineat up from the babysitter on our way back to my apartment from work. The children grew happier and more secure every day, because of all the love poured out upon them by kind friends.

Harold and Rena ended up helping me with the rest of the money I needed to get a car, and paid the insurance for a few months so I could begin driving!

When I filed for a divorce, I agreed not to ask for child support. Sorn had asked if I would do that, so he could work on paying off his debts. I asked for a court order requiring Sorn to leave me and children alone. Sorn had monthly visitation privileges with our three children, but he was ordered to stay at least one hundred feet from me when picking them up and leaving them off. However, the children were afraid of their father, and chose not to have him visit them. I was sad for him, but felt it was for the best.

The divorce was final in 1985, five years after arriving in America.

Things were falling into place. I had moved on, and my children and friends filled up all the spaces in my life. And as I grew in my knowledge of the Lord and his grace, I became content as never before in my life!

But I kept wondering about my parents and siblings. Were they alive? Were they wondering about me?

Chapter Twenty-Five

Longings

There were two things I continued to long for: to know what had happened to my family in Cambodia, and to find a church my children and I could attend. I prayed about both, with the hope that one day God would answer my prayers. While the children and I were out driving one Sunday morning, one of those prayers was answered!

I noticed a church not too far from where we lived in the foothills of Denver. It was a large church with four levels. I decided to stop and visit it. One of the church greeters who was standing in the foyer saw us come in, came over to us and shook all of our hands with a smile.

The size of the church was a bit overwhelming, and with four levels to choose from, I wasn't sure where we should go. Most of the people attending looked like typical Americans, and right away, I looked around to see if I could spot any of Asian descent so I could sit near them, but saw none.

I chose a level, and as I entered the auditorium, looking for a place with four seats, I had a definite 'wow-moment,' and said to myself, and I thought the church I first attended in Thailand at the refugee camp was large!

The following Sunday we returned, feeling a little less unfamiliar with our surroundings. We were greeted and welcomed once again and this time we learned the name of this huge building when one of the greeters said, "Welcome to Riverside Baptist Church."

What really thrilled me on that Sunday was to hear the three-hundred-member choir, singing 'Oh How I Love Jesus!' I had only known the name Jesus for a few years, and my love for Him was yet so new! One of the most faith-growing experiences I had was being a part of the worship team in that beautiful little open-sided, thatched roofed church in the Kam-Put Refugee Camp!

It was the choir that sold me! This will be my church, I told myself, and I started attending faithfully, and was soon making new friends at Riverside Baptist.

My first thought, after connecting with my new church, was to let the Williams know! But, that was impossible. I had received a letter from the Southern Baptist Organization to let me know that Wendy had joined Paul in heaven a year after her last visit to me in Denver. But who knows, I told myself, maybe they do know – maybe they're rejoicing with me that I am safe within Christ's body of believers here in Denver, at last! Were they in that great cloud of witnesses I'd read about in Hebrews 12?

Until this day I think of Paul and Wendy as my spiritual parents, even as Timothy thought of the Apostle Paul as his spiritual father. I'll always remember the morning I met Paul under the shady tree at the first refugee camp and heard in English about a man named Jesus that loved me. And I asked where I could go to see and talk to this man named Jesus. Paul was also the first person that mentioned the possibility of leaving Asia and immigrating to the United States.

I wonder what Paul would be telling me about heaven now that he's there? I asked myself. And then the Holy Spirit reminded me, you don't need Paul, Manith, you have a Bible that tells you all about it! A Bible you no longer have to hide!

But as God always does, he provided just what I needed: new mentors to take over where the Williams had left off. David Broughton was a deacon at Riverside, and his wife, Nancy, a member of that huge choir! This couple, David and Nancy Broughton, were to be my new guardian angels.

Nancy confided to me that they had never had children, and therefore, no grandchildren – and they'd decided to fill that spot in my children's lives – which pleased me very much!

I told the Boughton's that a Denver public school in our neighborhood was offering free classes to anyone who wanted to learn Spanish, and that I would like to take advantage of it. They were quick to offer their help. "Go ahead and sign up, Manith, we can watch your kids for you."

I already had four languages that I could speak with some fluency other than Cambodian: Laos, Thai, English and Vietnamese, and because so many people in the Denver area spoke Spanish, I thought this would open doors for me when I took jobs where they wanted someone who spoke Spanish.

They took my children into their hearts. And all three of my little ones grew close to them, especially Sineat, who by this time was starting first grade. She ate up the attention she got from Nancy and David. Almost every weekend we'd see them, and do something fun together.

We'd sing songs, play Bible games, go sight-seeing, or anything else that popped into our heads! We'd pile into their car and off we'd go on another exciting adventure!

David and Nancy knew the trails in the mountains that would be fun for us to hike. They showed us caves to explore, and even took us horseback-riding and would tell the children all kinds of stories about the wild west, making us feel like real westerners as we trotted about on our horses. The children learned more about American history and culture through them than they'd ever know before!

The Broughton's encouraged my growth in the Lord, and they introduced my children to the Awana Club that met on Wednesday nights – a club that emphasized learning Bible verses for badges.

It was explained to us how the club got its name: "AWANA is an acronym for a phrase in 2 Timothy 2:15, which says: Approved workmen are not ashamed."

The children were taught what that phrase meant: "The work we do when we are Christians is to read the Bible, and memorize key verses – and the more we memorize, the less ashamed we'll be. Do you know what King David said in Psalm 119:11?"

The children all shook their heads 'no' and the teacher quoted it: "Your Word I have hid in my heart, so that I won't sin against you."

"When we sin, do bad things, it makes us ashamed," she went on to explain. "But when we have Bible verses in our minds, it helps us not to sin! Then we are: approved workmen who are not ashamed!"

They got it, and all the children clapped their hands!

I joined the church choir, and it was delightful to sing new songs I'd never sung before with Nancy and the other members! And, as singing did for me in Thailand, my faith and commitment to the Lord grew stronger again, singing with this amazing choir.

Jesus was the fabric of my life, and he helped me as I stepped into being a single mom. I didn't feel so all alone now that I had a good church, and saw how the closer I got to the Lord, the closer

I got to my children and they to me. (That closeness has continued to this day, I always get flowers from them on Mother's Day and Father's Day.)

There is nothing that makes me happier than seeing smiles on my children's faces, and to realize how none of us would even be alive if it hadn't been for the Lord! I would remember having Punleu tied to my back, and Kamol tied to my breast, and myself tied to the man my dad had paid to lead us to the border of Thailand where we hoped to escape communism; and how I was led around death pits, and land-mines as we journeyed through Cambodia's jungles toward the Thailand border. Had we stepped on a land-mine, we would all have been killed immediately. I had not yet heard the name of Jesus, but he knew my name and was watching over us.

My children and I attended Riverside until they reached their teenage years. They were friends with the pastor's kids and sometimes had sleepovers. When I was just getting on my feet after leaving Sorn, it was the support, financially and spiritually, of Riverside Baptist that kept us going.

When my employers, Harold and Rena moved to Texas, I had to look for another job. They too had been guardian angels and had seen me through the horrible abuse years that led to my divorce, and I will always be grateful to them. I hated to see them go, but their investment in my life was not wasted. Because of a good work record, and their positive references, I didn't have a hard time finding another employment!

I was hired at an automobile company as a production supervisor – a job that I loved very much. It was having steady work and regular schedules that did a lot to keep our homelife strong, even in the most challenging of times.

We were always laughing. My kids loved telling me jokes they'd heard at school, or reminiscing about something funny that had happened in our family. When I laugh, I laugh so hard it makes my stomach hurt and tears come to my eyes, and when that happened, they loved it. We'd all go to bed happy after a good laugh – and less and less did the memories of going to bed in tears come to our minds.

Father, I would pray before falling asleep, you are always with me and my children, and my soul has so much peace now, and so few worries. Oh, thank you!

As the children got older, I realized we had outgrown our small apartment. And I began to save for a larger place – one that would give us more space.

I found a two-bedroom condominium about ten minutes from the company I worked for. I was now earning more money, and walking to work would save on gas, so, I told myself, this is going to work out very well!

Of course, it's a long way from church, I countered, but quickly agreed with my first assessment, but well worth the drive to be with new friends, have Awana for the kids, and to attend where the teaching focuses on the Lord Jesus!

A good evidence of the Lord's past guidance was that I had studied Spanish, because in my new job most of the workers were Hispanic. I could communicate with them very easily. Whenever new people were hired who only spoke Spanish, I would be called into the office to translate for them, and later when they were hired, take them through orientation.

And good evidence of God's daily guidance came when I had to decide whether to look for a Cambodian church in the Denver area, or to remain at Riverside where I had been attending for several months and had yet to meet another Asian in the congregation. At one point, I felt my Cambodian roots very strongly, and wanted to worship where I was understood, with people who knew what I'd been through and with whom I'd feel more at home, worshiping Jesus in my own language. I pondered this for a while, and then I reasoned (perhaps it was the Lord speaking to me): I need to be where I hear and speak English to become more fluent in the language of my new country. If I attend a Cambodian church, I'll develop spiritual vocabulary in my own tongue – but when I leave the church and rub shoulders with others who are not from Cambodia, I will be at a loss how to express in English the things that mean so much to me.

That made perfect sense, I told myself, wondering where all that wisdom had come from! I decided to stay right where I was – at Riverside Baptist!

I am in American, after all, I told myself, and need to become a part of the 'melting pot' – this country is made up of people from all over the earth who have come here for the freedoms it has to offer and I shouldn't be secluding myself with only Cambodians.

After making what turned out to be a very important decision, I ran into a friend of mine at the supermarket one morning. She looked so happy and said, "Hi, Manith! I have just become a citizen of America, and I'm having a party to celebrate my citizenship. Can you join us?"

I accepted her invitation. When I arrived, I saw lots of people and among them other Cambodians. I was curious about how my friend became a citizen of the United States, and I asked her about it.

"You've lived here for many years, Manith. I'd say this is now your country, and you should definitely consider becoming a citizen. The biggest advantage is that once you are a citizen you can legally sponsor others to come to the U.S.," she told me. "All you have to do is submit a Form N-400 application for Naturalization. It's a process that could take a year or two. There's a test you'll take, and lots to learn in order to pass it – the questions are mainly about U.S history and its government. When you pass, you will be given a notice to take the Oath of Allegiance to the United States, and that's what I just did, and why we are here celebrating today."

I went home that day and I knew that God had led me to stay on at Riverside – and that it would actually help me to prepare to become a U.S. citizen. What better place to practice speaking, reading, and thinking in English than in a church? Every sermon I heard forced me to think in English; every passage of scripture I looked up had to be read in English; every hymn or song I sang gave me an opportunity to think and speak in the language of this country! Free of charge, I was being given a good education in English by simply attending church.

I was as determined now to become a citizen, as I had been to immigrate to America when we were in Thailand! Thanks to my friend, and her instruction, I submitted the application, took the test, passed it, and now have my citizenship papers filed away; I can now vote for the president of my choice! What a far cry from communism – it's about as far as a person can get! Oh, that my physician uncle who was beheaded, my dear aunt who was burned, and my dear cousin that was chained, stabbed and thrown into a river could have come to America, too.

I became a U.S citizen in 1992. And then I began to search seriously for my parents and siblings so that, if they needed it, I could sponsor them to come to America and live with me.

Chapter Twenty-Six

A Call from Canada

Out of the blue, I received a phone call from Canada, of all places!

"Hello," spoke a woman's voice in Cambodian.

"Hello?" I responded, with questioning in my voice.

"Manith, this is Malyz Bour, your sister." I heard what she said, but couldn't believe it! It was like a dream, and for a while I didn't know how to respond!

"Malyz, is that you?" I asked.

"Yes, Manith, it is," she said. "Mom, Dad and most of our family live in Canada now."

"How did you get out of Cambodia?" I asked her. And she told me that she'd let me talk to our dad.

When I heard his voice, it was as though we had never been apart. If I closed my eyes, I could see myself as a girl, walking through his fields with him, admiring the crops we would soon be harvesting as a family!

We chatted for a few minutes and then I asked, "Papa, tell me about your escape. How did you get out of Cambodia!"

"After you left, Manith, we stayed for quite a while, but gradually the communists started pulling out of Sisophon and the surrounding jungles, and moved farther north. When they left, they took most of the soldiers with them that had been guarding the border into Thailand."

I interrupted and said, "Sorn told me that he returned to the village, and when he went to our house he found you all gone, and the house empty."

"Yes," my father answered, "for a long time we kept hidden in the jungles. And eventually, when we saw we could walk across the border into Thailand all together, we did, without any trouble. We went to the refugee camp expecting to find you and the children there, but could not locate you. We kept looking for you for two years, hoping you would show up, but finally gave up. The leadership in camp Khao-I-Dang went downhill. Bad things started happening. At night people would sneak into the camp to rob, and to rape the women."

"What did you do then?" I asked him.

"Someone told us that the Canadian government was accepting immigrants and we decided to apply for asylum. And in 1984 we were flown into Canada!"

"Did all of you leave Cambodia?" I asked him.

"No, your sister Manoeurn was married by the time we fled, and she stayed behind with her husband. She told us that someone had to stay near her grandmother's grave. But all of the rest came to Canada."

"How did you locate me and find my phone number?" I asked my father.

"I'll give you back to Malyz and let her explain that. Goodbye, my daughter," he said, and I almost cried to hear him call me *his daughter.*

"Hello, Manith, this is Malyz."

"Hello, Malyz. Tell me how you got my phone number."

"Well, one day I met a man in Toronto named Seth who was from Cambodia. He told me he had been in Kam-Put, the refugee transit camp in Thailand. And I asked him if he had ever met someone named Manith Bour. And he told me that he knew you. Not only that, he told me that you had immigrated to the U.S. in 1980, and I thought, *that's why we couldn't find her.* I asked him if he knew how to get hold of you, and he happened to have your phone number."

"Oh, Malyz," I told her, "That is unbelievable! You don't know how long I've been looking for you all. I've asked every Cambodian I have met here in Denver if they'd heard anything about my family."

I wanted a run down on all of my siblings, and I asked about them one by one. First I asked about my other sisters: Ny, Sitha, and Barang. And she told me how old they were now and what they were doing. And then she gave me a run-down on my little brothers: Sambath and Thourk!

We talked for a long time, and neither of us wanted to be the first to say goodbye! I think it was I, and when I did, I began to thank the Lord, with happy tears! I felt like a bird set free, and I knew that they were probably feeling the same way in Canada. We still call each other regularly. My mother has returned to Cambodia, and lives with my sister Manoeurn and her family in the same beautiful house in Sisophon that my dad built for us, with the balcony that goes around the whole house-on-stilts, near the grave of our beloved grandmother.

Malyz also told me that our father and mother never learned the languages of Canada – French and English, but that all of my siblings spoke both languages fluently.

I told Malyz that I too had learned two languages in my new country, English and Spanish.

I reminded her of how I alone among the children of our family had chosen education over farming, and how my first instruction in English was in high school, never dreaming I would be using it one day in America. We both remembered and repeated in unison what Grandmother would say: "Always take advantage of getting an education, so you can pursue good careers!"

(Little did grandmother know at that time, however, that following her advice is what put me on the LIST of the communists as *being too educated* to let live in the classless society they were trying to create in Cambodia.)

We also talked about the more light-hearted things – things that made us laugh! Malyz told me about the first time the family had gone out for hamburgers and how our mother had taken one bite and then rewrapped her sandwich, and thrown it in the garbage as soon as she got home, saying, "I'll never eat a hamburger again! I'd rather have rice!"

That reminded me of our first visit to a super-market, and how I'd asked the man from the immigrant facility who had taken us shopping, "How long has this meat had been dead!" That brought another fit of laugher from my sister Malyz.

She told me that some of my sisters had opened up their own spas, and nail salons, and were doing a good business. One of my brothers, she said, had married and the other was continuing his schooling. And that Dad became a 'handy-man' when they first arrived in Canada, and did odd jobs for people in the neighborhood who would hire him to fix fences, paint their homes, and things like that.

She wanted to know all about my children. And I told her how big Punleu and Kamol were now!

While talking with my Father, I mentioned that I'd given birth to another baby girl at the transit camp Kam-Put who we named Sineat.

"So, Sorn and you got back together again?" he asked.

I told him how Sorn came back into our lives in the refugee camp Khao-I-Dang, and how, when I saw how sick he was with tuberculosis, I didn't have the heart to turn him away after he found us.

"But as soon as he was well again, his abuse began," I told him. "The only times the abuse would stop was when we lived among others, but as soon as we were alone, it would start again."

And when I told him about the 28-day coma, and how I had almost died, I could tell he was shaken.

"You did right to divorce him, Manith," he said.

To hear him say that was such a relief! I had always hoped my parents would understand about the divorce.

"I would have left him much sooner, but I didn't want to dishonor you and my mother," I told him.

"You should have known that we would have protected you," he told me. "Like we did when you came back from Battambong to save the life of the baby in your womb. And again, when we paid the man who took you to the border, so that you could start a new life without Sorn in Thailand!"

There is no way to express the joy I felt to be back in contact with my family! My worries about them were gone! We were only a phone call away! I had a good job and three happy children!

How quickly my children embraced America and everything American – at school and at church they made friends with children of any race! Had I kept them surrounded by only Cambodians, they would not have been able to fit in like they have! Their knowledge of English quickly surpassed my own! I would still speak to them in Cambodian, and they would be able to understand some of what I said, but gradually lost their ability to speak it.

Not only did they prefer the language of their new land, they much preferred its food. They'd eat the Cambodian dishes I fixed for them, but when I'd order a pizza, that was special! Unlike their grandmother in Canada, who had declared thumbs down on all hamburgers, they loved MacDonald's hamburgers and French fries!

Time went by so fast! Punleu and Kamol finished high school, got jobs and helped me to support our family. I took a second job, and, with all of us working, I was able to get us an even bigger home.

And then, unbelievably, I was contemplating marrying again. Mutual friends at Riverside Baptist introduced me to Henry. He'd gone through a divorce just a year before we met, and no doubt, we were both rebounding from our failed marriages. We probably should have given it more time, but a short time after meeting, we married. He moved in with us, and at first we were happy, but nine months later, Henry was unfaithful to me and I asked him to move out. We divorced, and it was just me and the kids again.

I moved on with my life, deciding I would never again trust a man enough to marry him.

Sineat, the baby of the family, was in junior high the year after all of this took place. I concentrated on my children now, and was so proud of their accomplishments. When I'd hear them talking English so fluently, and doing so well, I felt such pride at how they were fitting in, and would tell myself, my children are smarter than I am! I will always be there for them, to support them in whatever they choose to do with their lives.

I've made some very bad choices, I would tell myself, *and I hope their futures will be more successful.* I wanted more for them that I had. I'd tried to give them a good start in the things of the Lord, and hoped, above all else, that they would become his children and serve him all their lives.

Eventually, Sineat and I had our two-bedroom house, with a one-car garage, all to ourselves. Punleu moved out to live on her own, and Kamol moved out a year later and moved in with a friend from high school. As graduation time grew closer, Sineat began talking about attending Arizona State College. The empty-nest was fast approaching.

They were all pursuing their own paths, but were good to keep in touch with me. I saw Punleu and Kamol often, and every month or so I would drive to Arizona to visit Sineat – the last to be born, but the first to marry.

After two years in college, Sineat walked in unexpectedly, dragging a man by the hand. With a big smile on her face, she introduced me to Isaac the man she was about to marry! She got right to the point. "We just got engaged."

They were married, and drove to the state of Maine where they'd found jobs. She had an independent spirit, and after marrying Isaac I rarely saw her – she was perfectly content on the east coast, living her life.

I lived by myself for seven years, and when loneliness set in, I bought a little Japanese puppy named Toby for company. He'd meet me at the door when I'd come home from work, and loved it when I took him for walks in the park after church on Sunday, what a comfort and joy he brought to my life! But something was still lacking!

I joined a Dance Club, and it was there that I first met Tony. Having experience two unhappy marriages, I enjoyed the dancing, but was determined not to get involved with any one.

We started out as good friends. There was a group of us who enjoyed being together, and I felt comfortable around Tony in a group setting. We danced together sometimes for a year or so and then, one day Tony asked to talk with me alone. I knew I could trust him and I agreed to a talk.

"Well, Tony," I said, "What was it you wanted to talk about?"

'I've been wondering," he started out, "How it works when a man falls in love with a woman of Asian descent and wants to marry her. Would they get married in Asian custom?"

"I didn't see this coming!" I said – not knowing if he was teasing or sincere. As our friendship grew from being just good friends to wanting to marry, I needed to counsel with someone – to get another perspective on things. So, I confided in my daughter Punleu.

"Tony has proposed to me and I'm scared," I told her, "I'm really not ready to commit to a marriage again, though I think a lot of Tony. Frankly, I'm feeling guilty. I've had two failed marriages. I've not been a very good role model for you children."

"Just the opposite," Punleu was quick to say. She helped me to see that I hadn't caused her father to be abusive, it had been his addictions, not mine, that had caused the marriage to fail. And I hadn't been unfaithful to Henry; he was the one who had been unfaithful to me. "You were actually a good role model, mother,

270

because you didn't permit the men you married to mistreat you. You were always thinking what was best for us children. And now you need to do what's best for you."

I also sought counsel from the Lord, and what I heard from Him was: keep praying, read my Word, remember that I love you and want you to be happy and at peace.

> "If any of you lack wisdom, let him ask of God, that gives to all men liberally, and upbraids not; and it shall be given him. But let him ask in faith, nothing wavering. For he that wavers is like a wave of the sea driven with the wind and tossed."

I reminded myself of the many times God had literally saved my life, and the fact that I was still alive was proof that I could trust him now to not let me down.

"Father," I would pray, "I don't know if I deserve another marriage. I love my life as it is now with freedom to worship you and serve you at my church. Lead me, and help me to know whether I should marry Tony."

I continued talking with all three of my children about it,

They were all in agreement that they wanted to see me with someone who loved and cared for me and who would be a good life partner. They were concerned about me being alone. "We are all on our own now, and It would be nice to know that when you are sick or need someone for whatever reason, there was someone to take care of you. You've been alone a long time now, Mother, maybe it's time your take your heart off the shelf and let Tony have it."

With their blessing, Tony and I were engaged in 2004, and my son Kamol let Tony know that my children welcomed him into our family. We started building our new home and made plans to get married.

I saw the Lord's hand in my feeling lonely enough to join the Christian Dance Club where single people from my church went on Saturday nights for entertainment. For it was there that I met Tony.

For many years I had lived a very limited life style as a single mom, trying at all times to live a life that would not harm me or my children, or cause me to be seen in a bad light. Worshiping the Lord, and attending church were the things that helped me at that time. I had neither time, energy, or finances for things other that our basic needs while raising my children.

And then, when my children moved on, God put people in my life that showed me for the first time what it was to relax and have fun! The Christian singles group went hiking, bike riding, fishing, camping and sometimes just walked around the lake as a group. With the ones I grew closest to, I went boating, sailing, water-skiing in the summer, and snowmobiling and dancing in the winter.

We were all in our thirties or forties, and a few a bit older. We all had the Lord in common, and it was a safe group to be with.

At first I didn't respond to Tony, not always because of the failed marriages, but just because I enjoyed being single and the freedom from responsibility to others. I loved the life I had with no more pressures. I didn't have to worry about making food for anyone or taking care of children.

My life as a single pleased me just fine. I kept busy with lots of activities. I wasn't looking for someone to marry, because I had good Christian friends to hang out with. Dancing kept me in shape and I never felt better physically. I loved to dance and would go every time I had the chance. I felt I had it all: friends that loved the Lord, a good job, and I'd found ways to serve the Lord! What more did I need.

Enter Tony! and the joys of singleness and entertainment faded!

He was a true blessing from the Lord. He showed me how much he cared for me; my children liked him and were willing for us to marry. My life would have been totally incomplete without him in it.

Our beautiful home was finished in 2005; it was there that we chose to be married – dressed in traditional Cambodia wedding clothes. Mother came from Canada, and joined my three children and the many friends who helped us to celebration both our marriage and our new home! Though my mother must have found our ceremony very quiet in comparison to my arranged marriage, when she had fed the whole village, but our marriage had her blessing as well as my father's and my siblings'!

Not quite a year later, Punleu gave us the good news that she would marry Courtney. My cup was full to overflowing. My two daughters were married, and both gave us grandchildren. We could see Court and Punleu who lived in Denver, and Kamol who had remained single. Sineat and I kept in touch by telephone.

Tony became a very good and loving stepfather and grandfather, who loved my children as his own. His love and support for me, set their minds at ease, and I cannot think of anything he would not do for them if they asked him.

We are thankful to the Lord for each of our children and our grandchildren. We pray for them each day, asking God to protect them and lead them into fellowship with himself, as he has us.

The day that we can say, our whole family knows the Lord, will be the happiest day of our lives! And we claim Acts 16:31 "Believe on the Lord Jesus Christ and you will be saved, *and all your house*."

I was so glad that Tony was in our lives when, about ten years ago, Punleu called to let us know that her father Sorn had passed away. It was a very sad time for our children. Tony stood with me, in comforting them. His steadiness helped us all.

And what has our marriage been like? A time of:

Sharing more and more stories about our pasts, so we can appreciate who we are today.

Making sure that the Lord is at the center of our marriage.

Being accountable to each other as we endeavor to be obedient to the Lord and to trust him at all times.

Being faithful not just to attend church, but to serve in our church.

To nurture our friendships by keeping in touch by phone, by texts, by emails.

To start each day with the Lord!

Chapter Twenty-Seven

A Story worth Telling

This book is the true story of an ordinary woman and an extraordinary God, his plans, and his people. The preceding chapters reveal God's mighty, mighty hand as, time after time, he saved my life from *Pol Pot's communism, and from the terrible abuse I went through during an arranged marriage. Though I am ordinary, the things I've written about were not ordinary happenings, and may have been disturbing to read. I wrote about them, not to shock you, nor to draw attention to myself, but to show what God can do for ordinary people like me when they go through things beyond their control. Throughout the world, ordinary people are still going through unbelievable sufferings today. I am convinced, however, from my own experiences, that God is everywhere, always present, *working all things together for good for those who love Him*, and in my case, even before I loved Him, because *He knows the plans He has for us, plans to prosper and not to harm us, but to give us a hope and a future!*

Even before I learned who He was, He was there. I believe that the comfort I felt at night lying close beside my baby daughter's little grave in the floor of our hut, was God comforting me. And I like to think, that while he was holding onto me, Kechara's little soul was in the tender hands of the One who invited little children to come unto Him when He was on earth!

Besides ordinary, there are two other terms that described me: fugitive and refugee.

As a fugitive, escaping in the black of the night through jungles to reach Thailand, I fell into a death pit with my little daughter Punleu strapped to my back, and my baby boy Kamol at my breast. The only thing that saved us was the rope that tied us to our guide. And how we avoided stepping on landmines, was because our guide was trained in spotting them!

I've learned that we are pilgrims and strangers in a dark world, where there are landmines and we need to be roped to our guide, the Lord Jesus, by faith in Him. Since He also walked through this world, He is good at spotting the landmines, and He can lead us around them.

My earthly 'guide,' however, left me on my own when we reached the barbed-wire barricade with bullets from machine guns zinging past my head. But my spiritual guide will never leave me or forsake me!

The Red Cross team met all who made it through the barricade, and changed our status from fugitive to refugee! They met us, cleansed us, treated our wounds, gave us blankets and a place to rest. We look to another Red Cross as we escape from the darkness of this world, and the one who hung upon it applies His blood, cleansing us from all our sins, and gives us rest for our souls.

> *That we might have strong consolation, who have fled for refuge to lay hold of the hope set before us.*
>
> *Hebrew 6:18*

When I was a slave of the communists, I did whatever I was told to do, and fear was my constant companion. I had to take a fake name, because my true name was on THE LIST. But when I made it through the barricade and the Red Cross worker asked my name, I could finally answer – Manith!

I would never have survived all I went through had not God gone before me – working in the hearts of people, prompting them to help me!

> *"The king's heart is a stream of water in the hand of the Lord; he turns it wherever he wills."*
>
> *Proverbs 21:1*

It's amazing to me that throughout my escapes and sufferings God used members of *PolPot's communist teams to help me – even at the risk of their own lives! *Kim, Reef, Mae* – all feminine communists – befriended me, shared secret information with me, and warned me to escape, and helped me to do it! I know for certain, it was God turning their hearts to do His will; I was a pawn in their hands and if they'd turned against me, I would have been killed!

Ean joined the communist cause to save his own life and to prevent them from finding out that his name was also on THE LIST. He knew his responsibility as a soldier was to kill me, but because of the God-planned-incident in high school when I had saved his life on a hike, he saved mine! Dismissing his soldier friends, he removed the black plastic bag from my head and helped me and the baby in my womb to escape with life!

Mr. and Mrs. Cong were also communists. Whether they joined *Pol Pot's communism to save their own lives or really believed in his dogma, I do not know, but their kindness to us when Sorn was near death, saved his life!

Seth made me a believer in how God uses "casual-encounters." We knew him only briefly in the transit camp in Thailand, but somehow we had ended up contacting each other by phone after he found asylum in Canada and we in the United States. And then, on another "casual-encounter" with my sister Malyz in Toronto, she, in the course of their conversation, mentioned she'd been trying to connect with her sister Manith. "Manith Bour?" Seth asked. And when she answered 'yes,' he said, "She's in the United States! And I have her phone number!"

God gave me spiritual parents, Paul and Wendy Williams. Throughout this book I've mentioned them over and over. With almost zero knowledge of the Cambodian, Laos, or Thai languages, they believed that God could use them to introduce Jesus to refugees from those countries. The miracle of their ministry was due to their simple faith in God's Word: *"And I, if I be lifted up from the earth, will draw all men unto me."* Paul told me that a man named Jesus loved me and that if I read the Bible, I could learn more about him. Which prompted my question, "Where is this Jesus? I want to meet him so I can thank him for loving me!" The Williams' put the Bible in our own languages into the hands of countless refugees, *expecting it to do its work*! And it did, in my case at least!

From fugitive to refugee to immigrant to citizen, I never lacked people to help and guide me!

I am sure God had much to do with my high school friend, A-Pichh, being accepted as an exchange student in the United States. It was how she escaped communism, and later on was there to sponsor me and my family when we were given asylum in America. *"The Lord is the one who goes ahead of you; He will be with you. He will not fail you or forsake you."*

Others who God put in my life to guide me were: Dr. Barns, who treated my injured foot for four years until it finally healed; Rena

278

and Harold, my employers, who took me and my children into their care after I spent 28 days in a coma; Cambodian friends who would rather remain anonymous, who hid me from Sorn and got me settled into an apartment with my children; the apartment managers, John and Maggie, who helped me with my children so that I could work; David and Nancy Broughton who befriended me and helped me when we attended Riverside Baptist; Adah who challenged me, and showed me how I could become a citizen of the United States.

And it goes on – after my marriage to Tony Sanchez – God had others in line to bless us as a couple!

Anita and Peter are neighbors and good friends. We love to get together with them! We gather around the fire pit that Tony built for us, and share stories and end up laughing or crying – confiding our joys and trials. We remind each other of the old songs we like and end up singing them together. And before we know it, we're talking about something we've read recently in the Bible. We're so grateful for the unique 'couple to couple' friendship we've had with them. Anita's soft voice reminds me of how soft and gentle the Lord Jesus is.

We've grown spiritually in each of the churches we've attended, but the biggest growth took place under the ministry of our mentor-pastor Ron Prosise and his wife Dona. The church he pastored was a community church with lots of activities, and we took advantage of them all.

Tony took part every month when the men would get together for *Bacon and Eggs and Bible* – iron sharpening iron. I loved seeing how connected my husband was with the men of the church! He began to grow in his faith and the more he served the Lord and others, the closer he felt to God!

We volunteered as a couple to cook for church-related events – like the appreciation days for Sunday School teachers or VBS (Vacation Bible School) Teams. Holiday banquets were fun, too – decorating tables and helping with the food provided good fellowship among those of us who worked on them. When fundraisers came around, we'd make and donate egg rolls! (My Asian background coming out!)

With others, we made and delivered food to new church members, and took meals to families who were sick or had new babies. Cooking was in my blood – and we made new friends by inviting people from church to come to our home for lunch or dinner.

Saturdays you'd find us taking our turns at trimming bushes and shrubs or mowing the lawn during the summer, and in the winter, getting there early to shovel snow so the people who walked into the church wouldn't slip and fall on the sidewalks.

It was fun for me to help with projects the women did, like creating a church cookbook, or just hanging out together for ice cream and Bible Study, led by the Pastor's wife, Dona.

When Ron and Dona left for another ministry in California, they often invited us to visit them! Ron insists it's for my cooking – but I know it's really for him to have another go at mentoring us. He will always be our forever pastor-mentor, and when trouble comes along in our marriage, we look to him and Dona for counsel and help!

When I met my mentor-mother, Maxine Morarie, her husband had already died after many years of suffering from Alzheimer's. During those hard years, his care took all her time and she hadn't done many things to decorate her home. One Christmas, her daughter, Carol Ann Kelly, our pastor Rob's wife at another church we attended, told Maxine that her gift for Christmas was going to be drapes! Carol Ann asked me if I would make the drapes for her mother, and that was our first contact!

I didn't really know Maxine, though I had no doubt seen her at church. You can imagine how surprised we were to learn that we both knew all about what it was to live in the jungles – she as a missionary in Bolivia, and I in my native country of Cambodia! When she told me that the Ayoré people she lived among had never before heard the name of Jesus, I said, "I can relate! I had never heard the name of Jesus either until I was married, had children, and was living in a refugee camp!"

In Cambodia, when someone becomes more like family than a friend, you call them brother or sister. In Maxine's case, after I bestowed the name of mother on her, I called her mama and she called me her girl! And when Tony's mother passed away, she took him into her heart and he became her son! We both came from large families, poor and needy at times. When she told me one day, that her mother had claimed that a good cook is someone that could make something out of nothing, we laughed, for we both have known what it is to make something out of nothing, ourselves.

No matter what I'm going through, I share it with Mama Maxine, and we see it through together. However long it takes, whether in person or on the phone, we talk it out, and then pray about it. I know my little sisters, Carol Ann and Tricia, mama's daughters, know I'm there for them if they need me. And when I clean my closet, I bag everything up and tell Mama to give it to them for their families!

It was she who inspired me to write this book. She understands, not only my somewhat broken English but also my heart! My sister Carol Ann typed my first efforts at a book, but Mama Maxine has taken my writings, interpreted them, sometimes adding her own two cents worth, and at last, this book has become a reality.

God has blessed Tony and I with seventeen years of marriage. There have been many trials – family matters, financial issues, marriage differences, but in them all, we've learned so much about each other as husband and wife, and our first and foremost goal is to love Jesus together, and as individuals. My closest mentor is Tony – I've learned so much from him, and I look forward to his daily texts and calls from work – assurances that he is thinking about me! And if I've 'rubbed off on him' it's probably because I appreciate him so much, and delight to cook his favorite dishes! Tony has loved me and grown in the Lord with me, and we're so thankful for our years together.

And speaking of mentors, JESUS is the greatest mentor of all. He has placed his very own Spirit in my heart and that Spirit brings to my mind his words – just when I need them most! And while I was yet without any knowledge of him, he was seeking me and helping me to find him. He protected my true identity from the communists who had written my name on their LIST as someone to be killed. He brought me to safety where I learned the name above all names, and when I believed in him, I was put on another LIST as someone who should live forever!

And because the love of God is now shed abroad in my heart, at last, I am able to forgive those who pursued me, persecuted me, and used me as a slave. I forgive those who killed my uncle, my aunt, and my cousin, and those who withheld the medications that could have saved my first-born baby. I forgive and honor my husband Sorn, for being the father of our four beautiful children, even though his weaknesses led to cruel abuse.

I have to admit, though, that sometimes revenge still crops up in my heart, and I want the perpetrators punished for the killing fields, the death pits, the mistreatment of elderly people, for robbing Cambodia's youth of their innocence, erasing compassion and conscience from their hearts and using them to kill and dismember the bodies of thousands and thousands and thousands of innocent victims!

But then, in my mind, I see Jesus, with a crown of thorns on his head, nails in his hands and feet, thirsty and bleeding on the cross, and I hear him saying, *Father, forgive them, they know not what they do!* And I hear the Bible speaking to my heart: *Dearly beloved, avenge not yourselves: for it is written, Vengeance is mine; I will repay, saith the Lord.*

The pre-communist Cambodia that I knew as a child was so beautiful and that is the country I prefer to remember, not what it became. I have not wanted to return to the land of my birth, lest, seeing how it has changed, I lose the sweet memories I've tried to hang onto.

My father has departed this life, but before his death, he went back to Cambodia for visits. And my mother is now living in Sisophon with my sister. My siblings also have paid visits to their country of origin, and have urged me to do so, as well. I have discussed going back with Tony many times, but only two places draw me: Sisophon where I could visit Grandmother's grave, and the village where Kechara is buried. I know I could never locate her little grave, for the whole village was burning as I was fleeing from it, but perhaps even being in the vicinity would be a way of honoring the little one I buried with my own hands.

But Jesus is the fabric of my life now, and I leave everything in His hands. May I close by thanking him for all he's done for me?

> I thank you, Lord Jesus, that I literally *saw a thousand fall at my side, and ten thousand at my right hand,* but I did not perish in a pit!

> I thank you that even though I stepped on a rusty nail and almost suffered an amputation of my foot, *you gave your*

angels guard over me and I'm still walking around on my own two feet!

I thank you that I have your assurance that *no evil shall befall me, no plague will come near my dwelling.*

I thank you that I arrived in the United States with nothing in my hands, but you have filled them full with all I could ever need or want.

I thank you that *your mercies are new every morning* and I ask those mercies for my family, that you will bring each one – my mother, my siblings, my children, and my grandchildren – to yourself, just as you have brought me. May they ask you to be their God instead of the Buddha that some of them still worship.

I thank you that I am no longer a fugitive, running and escaping from one place to another to stay alive.

I thank you that, although I'll always miss my baby Kechara, my Uncle, my Aunty, and my Cousin, I no longer cry for them, because you have healed my sorrow.

I thank you that I live in freedom as a citizen of the United States of America that gave me asylum.

I thank you for my sisters in Christ like: Wendy Williams, Alice Dodge, Dona Prosise, Anita Sanchez, Bong Noeurn, women who sat beside me and encouraged me many times.

I thank you for my brothers in Christ like: Pastor Ron Prosise, Bong Phal Chhith, Paul Williams (who is now with the Lord).

I thank you for my mama Maxine who inspired me to write my book, and has helped me all the way with her editing and ghost-writing.

I thank you for my honorary sister Carol Ann Kelly who took my hand-written journals and typed them into the computer, and who will take this manuscript and tweak it for me.

I thank you for my honorary sister Tricia Lee Jolly who has asked for a copy to read.

I thank you for Britney Farr who, despite her busy schedule, was willing to work with me on my book.

I thank you for Jake Brown, a published author, who has agreed to read my manuscript.

I thank you for my beloved husband Tony who has stood by my side, encouraging me to keep on writing.

I thank you, Lord Jesus, that I can talk with you anywhere at anytime. No matter what happens to me in this world, *I will wait upon you, and rise up with wings like an eagle, I will run and not be weary and I will walk and not faint.*

May all who read my story know that it doesn't cost anything to ask Jesus into our hearts, yet he gave his all for us. He's left us the promise of his continuing presence - he'll never leave us or forsake us. Everything else in life will grow old and wear out, but Jesus stays the same yesterday, today, and forever. He loves us – we can safely trust him.

> *From the rising of the sun unto the going down of the same the LORD'S name is to be praised. The LORD is high above all nations, and his glory above the heavens. Who is like unto the LORD our God, who dwelleth on high, and humbles himself to behold the things that are in heaven, and in the earth!*
>
> *Psalm 113:3*

*Pol Pot (born Saloth Sar; May 19, 1925–April 15, 1998) was a Cambodian dictator. As the head of the Khmer Rouge, he oversaw an unprecedented and extremely brutal attempt to remove Cambodia from the modern world and establish an agrarian utopia. While attempting to create this utopia, Pol Pot initiated the Cambodian genocide, which lasted from 1975 to 1979 and caused the deaths of at least 1.5 million Cambodians.

Michael Richards,
Contributing Writer,
Updated May 22, 2019

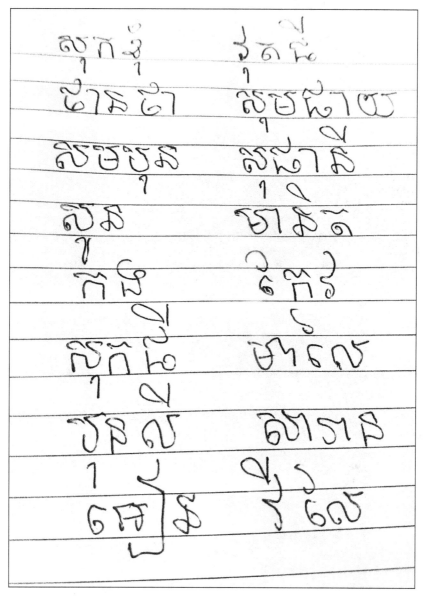

Cambodian list

287

Baptism

Bong Phal and his wife.

Church

Family

Mama Maxine

Parents and Siblings

My 3 children

Paul and Wendy.

Wedding Photo

The Prosise couple

About the Author

My name is Manith Sanchez (Maiden Manith Khoun) and I was born in Sisophon, Cambodia. I lived in this beautiful country until the age of 19. Never would I have imagined the horrifying events that would take me to the point of no return. But by God's grace, He has given me a life of joy and happiness. I am a wife, mother of three children - three girls and one boy. I am a grandmother of six grandchildren. All of whom I love so much and I am blessed by God to have them in my life. I love to cook. I cook a lot of Asian foods such as, Cambodian, Vietnamese, and Thai just to name a few. I love serving in my church and serving in the community. I wrote this book to encourage people from all

walks of life, that no matter what happens, with perseverance and determination you can survive in this world. But most important by having Christ as your Lord and Savior, He can bring you through adversity, and walk with you every step of the way. I am living proof of this.

CPSIA information can be obtained
at www.ICGtesting.com
Printed in the USA
BVHW030058170722
641969BV00003B/12